A FIGHTING FRIGATE

AND OTHER ESSAYS AND ADDRESSES

A FIGHTING FRIGATE

AND

OTHER ESSAYS AND ADDRESSES

BY

HENRY CABOT LODGE

Essay Index Reprint Series

BOOKS FOR LIBRARIES PRESS
FREEPORT, NEW YORK

First Published 1902
Reprinted 1969

STANDARD BOOK NUMBER:
8369-1222-5

LIBRARY OF CONGRESS CATALOG CARD NUMBER:
79-90655

PRINTED IN THE UNITED STATES OF AMERICA

TO

WINTHROP MURRAY CRANE

Governor of Massachusetts

You will find in this volume three addresses upon the lives and public services of three Governors of the State of Massachusetts who were your friends as well as mine. I have reprinted these addresses here because the careers of these Massachusetts Governors seem to me to have been an honor to their State and country. To you, their successor, wholly worthy to stand with them among the most eminent of the long and distinguished line of the Chief Magistrates of Massachusetts, I dedicate this book. I ask you to accept it as a mark of my personal regard and of my admiration for your wisdom, your character, and your ability, as well as for the high and disinterested principles of conduct by which you have been guided in your most efficient and successful public service.

TABLE OF CONTENTS

A FIGHTING FRIGATE [1]

THE United States frigate Constitution has come back to Boston and to Massachusetts. She floats again upon the waters into which she rushed as she left the builder's ways a hundred years ago. She returns to us stripped of her masts and spars, of her sails and guns, of all that once made her a thing of life. She is little more now than a hulk, roofed over and weather-beaten, helpless and motionless on the sea where once she rode triumphant. Curious inquirers have been at pains to tell us that of the ship launched in 1797 scarcely anything remains; that in her long career she has been made over from truck to keel. So be it. Whether the statement is true or false matters not. It is not a given mass of wood and iron which touches our hearts and stirs our pride. It is the old ship herself, because she is the visible symbol of a great past, charged with noble memories, and representing sentiments, aspirations, and beliefs far more lasting than

"Brass eternal, slave to mortal rage."

[1] Address delivered in the Old South Church, Boston, October 21, 1897, on the occasion of the return of the frigate Constitution to the Charlestown Navy Yard.

1

That which concerns us here is what this old man-of-war means to us, not what she is. There is "much music, excellent voice" in this historic ship, and, more fortunate than Hamlet's friends, we know the touch of it and can make it speak.

Every one is familiar with Turner's famous picture of "The Fighting Temeraire Towed to her Last Berth." It is a masterpiece of England's greatest painter. The splendor of the execution arrests the eye at once. The crowded river, the disturbed water, the smoky mist, the marvellous effects of clouds and color, of light and shade, all fill the gazer with wonder and delight. But there is much more than this. As we look at the old brown hulk dragged slowly up the murky stream, we see that the canvas before us is not only a picture, but a poem full of pathos and of memories. The old ship's course is run. She will never face the seas nor front the foe again. The end of a great career, always pathetic to the finite mind, is here very present to us. Yet even this is not all which genius has put upon the canvas. Turner was painting more than water, sky, and ship. He has touched the scene with the enchanter's wand, and we behold as in a magic mirror the story of England's navy. The long roll of her sea fights stretches out before us. All the great figures are there, from Grenville sinking on the Revenge ringed round by foes, and Blake burning the Spanish ships at Cadiz and sweeping through the Mediterranean, to Nelson dying victorious at Trafalgar. Above all, the "Fighting Temeraire" speaks to us of that supreme period of England's naval history when she had crushed France and Spain, and ruled the ocean unopposed, the great sea power of the world. Against that mighty power, in the full flush of victory and dominion, we took up arms, and England suddenly discovered that, ship for ship and man for man, she had more than met her match.

It was by no fault of their own that the United States found themselves pitted in a terribly unequal struggle against this great antagonist. From the renewal of the Napoleonic wars, after the rupture of the Peace of Amiens, there was no insult, no humiliation, no outrage which the two great combatants, England and France, failed to inflict on the United States. The administrations of Jefferson and Madison attempted to meet these attacks with diplomacy, which was worthless, because not backed by either courage or force, and with commercial restrictions which injured us more than those against whom they were aimed. On the other hand, the Federalist opposition, sympathizing with England in her struggle against Napoleon, taunted the administration with the humiliations to which we were forced to submit, and yet made a factious resistance to every effort at retaliation. Gradually the situation grew too intolerable to be borne. If our flag was to be flouted, our seamen impressed, our ships seized, our diplomatists insulted, then our independence for which we had fought was a delusion, and we were abject slaves of a worse tyranny than any ever dreamed of in colonial days. This the spirit of the American people could not endure, and a new party rose up, led by Clay, Calhoun, and the younger men of the South and West, who determined that we should at least vindicate our right to exist as a nation, and that it was better to go down fighting, if sink we must, than to submit to degradation and ruin without a murmur. This new party meant to fight. That they rushed forward blindly, that they counted no cost, that they were guilty of loud boasting without making any preparation, that they allowed words to pass for deeds, when what we needed were soldiers, sailors, and ships, and not language, is all sadly true. And yet none the less were they fundamentally right. At that period, if we were to have peace or honor or national existence, we were compelled to fight. The new war party did not care with whom we fought. They were ready to fight both France and England, or either of them. There was not much to choose so far as their ill-treatment of us was concerned, and it was indeed merely owing to the cynical duplicity and mendacity of Napoleon that we finally went to war with England instead of with France. Into that conflict the new party dragged the reluctant President, while the Federalists, with bitter if unconscious satire, called it "Mr. Madison's war."

Thus war began. We were utterly unprepared on land. At the time of the Revolution a large part of the people lived on the frontier, and were pioneers, backwoodsmen, and Indian fighters. Even in the older settlements, except in a few seaport towns, the men from their boyhood were accustomed to shoot and ride. Their habits of life were such that they were easily made into soldiers, for they were riflemen and horsemen naturally, and lacked nothing but drill and discipline. In 1812 the growth of the country had changed the situation. We had no organized militia, as we have to-day, and soldiers had to be taken largely from among men who had never fired a gun or mounted a horse. We could not make an army out of this material as quickly as we did in the Revolution. Yet the bravery and fighting capacity of the race are shown by the fact that in two years we had soldiers able to fight with the best at Lundy's Lane and Chippewa, while the Spaniards, after five years of service under Wellington, raced away at Toulouse as if they had never seen an enemy. None the less, the two years spent in making soldiers after hostilities had begun were marked by disasters which suitable preparation for war would have avoided.

At sea the case was very different. The last
Federalist Administration had begun our naval policy,
and built ships of the finest types. The policy was
abandoned by Jefferson, but the ships remained, and,
although they were few, they were of the best. We
were a seafaring people, and the American sailor became a man-of-war's-man at once. At sea, therefore,
although in a very limited way, we were prepared,
and the result was at once apparent. The career
of the Constitution illustrates that of the American
navy throughout the war, although she was not only
uniformly victorious, but more fortunate than many
of her sister ships in escaping capture by a superior
force. To tell the splendid story of the Constitution in the detail it deserves would take hours, and
to-day we have only minutes to give.

I can only touch here very briefly on the events which
have made the old ship so famous. Commanded by
Capt. Isaac Hull, she left the Chesapeake on the 12th
of July, 1812. On the 17th she almost ran into a
British squadron, consisting of a ship of the line of
sixty-four guns and four frigates. They gave chase.
For three days, through perilous calms, when he
towed and warped his ship along, through light and
baffling breezes, through squalls and darkness, Hull
worked his way until the last enemy dropped below the horizon. It was a fine exhibition of cool
courage and skilful seamanship. He outmanœuvred

and outsailed his foe, and escaped from an over-
whelming force flying the flag of the mistress of the
seas. July 26 the Constitution reached Boston, and
on August 2 set sail again, and stood to the eastward.
Thence she went to the Bay of Fundy and ran along
the coast of Nova Scotia and Newfoundland to Cape
Race. On the 19th she sighted the Guerrière, one
of the ships which had pursued her, and bore down
at once. There was an hour of long-range firing,
by which little damage was done, and then the
Constitution closed, and they exchanged broadsides
within pistol shot. The sea was very rough, but the
American aim was deadly. The Constitution was
but little damaged, while the Guerrière's mizzenmast
went by the board. Then Hull luffed under his enemy's
bows and raked her, then wore and raked again. So
near were the two ships now that they became entangled. Boarders were called away on the Guerrière,
but the British recoiled from the mass of seamen on
the American ship. The sea indeed was so high that
boarding was impossible, although the Americans tried
it, and the musketry fire at these close quarters was
very severe. Then it was that the Americans suffered
the loss of the day, but that of the British was much
heavier. Finally the sea forced the ships apart, after
this brief hand-to-hand conflict, and as they separated
the foremast and mainmast of the Guerrière went by
the board, so that she rolled a helpless hulk upon the

waves. Hull drew off, repaired damages and bore down again, when the Guerrière struck her flag. The next day Hull took off all her crew, and the Guerrière, shot to pieces and a mere wreck, was set on fire and blown up. We had a better ship, more men, and threw a greater weight of metal. But we also fought our ship better and were better gunners, for while the Constitution lost fourteen killed and wounded, the Guerrière lost seventy-nine, and was herself utterly destroyed.

Hull returned in triumph to Boston, and the news of his victory filled the country with pride, and England with alarm. The London "Times" thought it a serious blow to England's naval supremacy. "It is not merely that an English frigate has been taken," said the "Times," "but that it has been taken by a new enemy." At that period England naturally enough considered herself invincible. Her officers and seamen never stopped to consider odds, but closed with an antagonist and then romped on board her, confident that one Englishman was equal to at least five Frenchmen or Spaniards. The results hitherto had justified their confidence, but now sprang up a people who had faster ships, sailed better, and shot straighter than they, and who were also quite as ready as they to come to close quarters by boarding. One frigate was nothing, but the facts flashed out in this first fight of the Constitution were impressive.

Hull resigned the command of the Constitution, and was succeeded by Captain Bainbridge, who sailed on October 26. In December the Constitution was off the coast of Brazil, and just as the year was closing she fell in with the Java, carrying out Lieutenant-General Hislop, the new Governor of Bombay. The Java was one of the crack frigates of the British navy. She was faster than the Constitution, and carried only 50 less men, and 78 pounds less weight of metal. The ships were thus pretty evenly matched, and the Constitution suffered most from the first broadside exchanged at long range. After that, however, the British fire was steadily inferior, while that of the Americans became more and more deadly. Captain Lambert, who was killed in the action, handled his ship with skill and fought her with the utmost gallantry. But, despite the Java's advantage in speed, Bainbridge's admirable seamanship overcame it, and he kept clear of being raked by wearing in the smoke, although his wheel had been shot away and his steering was hampered. The Java getting more and more crippled and suffering severely from the fire from the American tops, Captain Lambert ordered her to be laid aboard the enemy. She came down with her men ready for the spring, but before she reached her antagonist her maintopmast and her foremast had been shot away. Her bowsprit caught in the Constitution's mizzen rigging, and the Americans raked her once more. Again the ships swung side by side, but the American fire tore the Java to pieces, and finally silenced her guns. The Constitution bore up, spent an hour in repairing damages, and then stood again toward the Java, only to have her strike her colors. Two days later Bainbridge took the crew out and destroyed his prize, for she was too much injured to be carried to the United States. It had been a hard-fought action between two nearly equal antagonists, and the British lost their ship and 150 men in killed and wounded, while the Americans' loss was 48. Each captain fought his ship well, but it was the precision and rapidity of the American fire which won the day and inflicted such disproportionate loss on the enemy.

The Constitution continued in active service, doing good work and escaping capture by superior force, but it was not until 1815, after peace had actually been signed, that she won her last victory. Commanded by Capt. Charles Stewart, she slipped out of Boston Harbor on December 17, 1814, and on February 20, off Madeira, fell in with the frigate-built corvette Cyane and the sloop Levant. They were ready enough to fight, and, the Constitution coming up with them soon after six o'clock, the action began at close quarters with both the enemy's vessels on the port side of the frigate. The broadsides were heavy and continuous and the firing from the tops steady. This lasted a quarter of an hour. It was then moonlight, and a heavy cloud of smoke hid the British vessels. Stewart therefore stopped firing, and when the smoke lifted he saw the Levant dead to leeward and the Cyane luffing up for his port quarter. He braced his topsails back, backed rapidly astern, forcing the Cyane to fill to avoid being raked, and then poured in his broadsides. The Cyane's fire slackened and died away. The Levant coming to the rescue, Stewart drove her off with two broadsides and fell again upon the Cyane, which struck just before seven o'clock, after an action lasting forty minutes. Putting a prize crew on the Cyane, Stewart bore down after the Levant, which first fought, then tried unsuccessfully to escape, and finally struck. Stewart sailed with his prizes to the Cape de Verde Islands, and while there at anchor sighted three heavy British frigates making for the harbor. He at once, with a rapidity which showed the remarkable skill and discipline of his crew, got all three vessels under way and put to sea. The Cyane escaped and was brought safely to the United States. The Constitution also outsailed her pursuers, but the Levant took refuge in Porto Praya, and as England did not pay the slightest attention to the neutral rights of a weak power, was there recaptured. This action was one of the most brilliant bits of seamanship and manœuvring in the whole war, for Stewart not only defeated two antagonists, but captured them both. The British had 130 less men and 59 pounds greater weight of metal than the Constitution, yet they lost fifty-seven men and both ships. It was a fit close to the career of the Constitution, which had never lost a fight or been caught by a superior force.

I have touched only on the exploits of the Constitution in the War of 1812, and have not recounted at all the work she did in checking the attacks of the French at the close of the previous century or the large part she took in the war with the Barbary States, when under Preble she bombarded Tripoli and imposed submission on that nest of pirates. But creditable as were those earlier performances, it was only in the War of 1812 that the career of the Constitution takes on a wide importance and a deep significance. She may stand for us as the exemplar of the American navy at that period, and it was the work of the navy which then vindicated our national existence and relieved us forever from the state of oppression and outrage to which we had been subjected. In saying this I do not overlook the good fighting that our soldiers finally did on the Canadian border. Still less do I forget New Orleans. Jackson, drawing on a population of frontiersmen and Indian fighters of the same class as those who in the Revolution had crushed Burgoyne and won King's

Mountain, found material ready to his hand out of which an army could be quickly developed. With six thousand American riflemen he defeated with heavy loss more than ten thousand of Wellington's Peninsula veterans, who had swept before them the soldiers of Napoleon, commanded by one of the ablest of his marshals. But New Orleans was fought after the peace had been signed. It did not affect the outcome of the war, and English histories would seem to indicate that the news of Jackson's victory was never received, nor the facts in regard to it ever known, in England. The fighting which brought us out of the war with an unsatisfactory treaty, but with every substantial object fully attained, was that of the lakes and the ocean. Perry's victory on Lake Erie, and MacDonough's less famous but equally important and more brilliant victory at Plattsburg, won against odds with which Perry did not have to contend, rendered all the military successes of the British of no avail. This was acknowledged by Wellington, who, when he was asked to take command in America, said that if he went out it would only be to make peace, for he did not see that England had achieved any success which could compel from the Americans the slightest concession of territory or principle.

On the ocean our victories in material results were trifling, but their effect was enormous. It was not

that we had taken a few frigates, preyed successfully
on British commerce, and raised insurance rates in
London, but that we had demonstrated to the world
that we were formidable fighters, capable of contest-
ing the dominion of the seas with any power, and if
pushed to the wall, able to wreck the trade and commerce of our antagonist.   We went into the contest
with some dozen men-of-war, while England had a
thousand.   The few sloops and frigates which England lost to us were in themselves hardly to be
noticed in the immense mass of her naval force.
But the moral and political effect was incalculable.
A single brief statement shows what the American
victories meant. In twenty years England had
fought over two hundred single ship actions, with
pretty much every people of Europe, and had lost
only five of them.   In six months she fought five
single ship actions with us and lost every one.   During the war, despite the fact that our ships, as was
inevitable, were sooner or later taken or blockaded
by vastly superior force, there were thirteen single
ship actions, including that of the Constitution with
the Cyane and Levant, and England won two and
lost eleven.   To the great sea power of the world
these facts were grave and alarming.   At the same
time, also, our cruisers and privateers ranged the
English Channel and swarmed along the highways of
ocean traffic, harrying and capturing British mer-

chantmen and forcing up insurance to a height unheard of before. A few pointless raids and barren
victories in America were all Great Britain could set
against these painful losses of ships and money. In
a word, her naval prestige was damaged, and her
commerce injured by a new sea power, rapidly developing under the stress of war. There was no way
to get compensation for such vital wounds as these
from a nation three thousand miles away. Hence
the treaty of Ghent. Hence the vindication of the
rights of the United States as a nation.

That this is a correct statement of the effect of the
fighting done by the Constitution and her sister ships
is proved not only by our own opinion, but by that of
England and Europe as well. Sir Howard Douglas,
in his book on gunnery, which for fifty years was the
text-book of the English Navy, takes nearly every
example of single ship actions from our War of 1812.
There we may learn that it was the Americans who
first taught the naval world to fire on the falling
wave, which at that day was little less than a revolution in practical gunnery. If we turn to the greatest
of the French naval authorities, Admiral Jurien de la
Gravière, an entirely disinterested witness, we shall
find that almost the only single ship actions which
he mentions are ours. He gave as much attention
to them as to the great fleet actions of the preceding
twenty years, and he was writing a purely scientific

book on naval warfare for the French. These high
authorities, one French and one English, prove that
in single ship actions, which alone we were able to
undertake, we at once went to the front rank, surpassed even England, and gave lessons in seamanship
and gunnery to the great sea power of the world.

The moral effect of our victories and of our sea
fighting is shown even more strikingly by contemporary opinion. In 1827 James, the English naval
historian, wrote as follows to George Canning: "The
menacing tone of the American President's message
is now the prevailing topic of conversation, more
especially among the mercantile men, in whose company I daily travel to and from town. One says,
' We had better cede a point or two than go to war
with the United States.' ' Yes,' says another, ' for
we shall get nothing but hard knocks there.' ' True,'
adds a third; ' and what is worse than all, our seamen are more than half afraid to meet the Americans
at sea.' Unfortunately this depression of feeling,
this cowed spirit, prevails very generally over the
community; even among persons well informed on
other subjects, and who, were a British seaman to
be named with a Frenchman or a Spaniard, would
scoff at the comparison." About the same time
Stratford Canning came out as Minister to the
United States. He was a man of ability and of
high and imperious temper, very well known after-

ward as Lord Stratford de Redclyffe, the "Great
Eltchi" of the Eastern question, and the chief author
of the Crimean War. He was sent here through the
influence of his cousin, George Canning, then a member of the Ministry, — the same George Canning who,
in the first decade of the century, had sneered at and
trampled on the United States, and called our navy
"a few fir frigates, with bits of bunting at the top."
Since that jeer had been flung at us these "fir
frigates" had whipped British frigates in every
action fought by them but one, and when the imperious and somewhat domineering Stratford Canning came to Washington he wrote as follows of
his purpose: "The maintenance of peace was to
be my principal care, and with this view it was de-
sirable that I should be rather observant than active,
slow to take offence, and in the management of current affairs more tolerant of adverse pretensions than
ready to push my own claims to an extreme." Mr.
Poole, Stratford Canning's biographer, adds: "Con-
ciliation was then the purpose of the British Government, — England had learned by more than one
experience that the temper of the states was not to be
rashly trifled with." What a change of tone is here
from that of the early years of the century, when the
words and actions alike of foreign Powers toward
the United States are such that we cannot recall
them even now without a hot blush of shame and

mortification! What a good lesson had been taught, and how much had really been done for peace by the guns of that old ship now fallen silent forever!

Another little incident in this same direction is also very suggestive. At almost his first interview with Stratford Canning, John Quincy Adams, then Secretary of State, said, "It took us last time several years to go to war with England; it would only take several weeks now;" and Mr. Canning accepted the intimation in good part. Mr. Adams has been dead for more than fifty years, and he may safely, therefore, be called a statesman, and a great one, too, whose opinions it is well to heed. A little reflection, moreover, will show that he was entirely right in his attitude toward England, and in reality the best friend and maintainer of peace. Jefferson and Madison were hesitating and timid. They swallowed insult in the interests of peace and landed us in war. Mr. Adams took a high, firm tone with England and maintained peace inviolate. Jefferson and Madison abandoned ship building, prepared no defences, and drifted, feebly gesticulating, into a conflict with the greatest sea power of the world. John Quincy Adams and Andrew Jackson after him took a strong and self-respecting tone with all the world and kept an unbroken peace. England and Europe received valuable instruction from the war of which this battered old ship is the sign and symbol, but we Americans were taught a great deal more. We had learned that weak defencelessness meant war, and strong, armed readiness meant peace, honor, and quiet. When John Quincy Adams spoke to Mr. Canning he knew that he was backed by a strong navy, for in 1826, with a population of ten millions, we had a larger navy than we have to-day,[1] with a population of seventy millions. It is well to note that the lesson of wise preparation, taught by the War of 1812, and always worth remembering, is even more important now than then, for to-day great wars are fought in a few months, while it takes years to build modern ships and cast rifled guns.

Out of the War of 1812 came these teachings, and out of these teachings, taken to heart, as they were, by the men of that day, came peace, the only peace worth having. One hears it often said by persons who are prone to mistake for thought the repetition of aged aphorisms, that some people intend to have peace even if they fight for it. They imagine that they are giving utterance to a biting and conclusive sarcasm, when in reality they are stating a profound and simple truth. All the peace the world has ever had has been obtained by fighting, and all the peace that any nation, which is neither subject nor trivial,

[1] The American navy has not only done some fighting quite in the fashion of 1812, but has been much increased since these words were spoken in 1897.

can ever have, is by readiness to fight if attacked.
In our cities and towns we maintain a large army
of soldiers.   We call them policemen, but they are
drilled and organized, and are in all essentials a
military body.   For what purpose are they maintained ? To make war on any one ? On the contrary,
we have police in order to keep the public peace.   In
the same way must the peace of nations be kept.
Weakness, fear, and defencelessness mean war and
dishonor.   Readiness, preparation, and courage mean
honor and peace.   Where we were unprepared
in 1812 we suffered ; where we were prepared we
prospered and vindicated our national existence.
That is the true line of national policy for which
the Constitution stands to-day just as much as
when she overcame the English frigates.   Her builder,
building better than he knew, both in timber and in
words, called her with a fine eloquence " a powerful
agent of national justice."   So she was, and she was
also a minister and guardian of peace, — not the
peace at which a spirited people revolts, but the
peace of which Lowell sings :

> " Come peace ! Not like a mourner bowed,
>   For honor lost an' dear ones wasted,
>   But proud, to meet a people proud,
>   With eyes that tell o' triumph tasted."

But there is still something more in this ship
Constitution than vivid instruction as to the truest

national policy. She is the yet living monument, not alone of her own victories, but of the men behind the guns who won them. She speaks to us of patriotism and courage, of the devotion to an idea and to a sentiment for which men laid down their lives. The distinguished President of a great university has recently warned his students against the tendency " to magnify the savage virtues." It is well recognized that certain virtues can be carried to a point where they cease to be such, but it is not quite clear how a genuine virtue of any kind can be too much magnified. The virtues termed " savage " I take to be the early and primary ones of courage, indifference to danger, and loyalty to the tribes or clans which, in the processes of time, became nations and countries. These primary or " savage " virtues made states and nations possible, and in their very nature are the foundations out of which other virtues have arisen. If they decay, the whole fabric they support will totter and fall.

The gentler virtues, as well as the refinements and graces of civilization, rest upon these simpler qualities, and the highest achievements of the race in the arts of peace have come from the strong, bold nations of the earth. Art, literature, philosophy, invention, in Greece and Rome, in Venice and Holland, all reached their zenith when those countries were at the height of their military and political power, and sank as that power decayed. The discoveries, the education, the freedom, the material development, the vast growth of all which is required to raise and to better the conditions of mankind, have been most conspicuous and have made the largest progress among those nations which were strongest, most daring, and readiest to defend their rights. Material success with all that it implies is a great achievement, but it is as nothing to the courage and faith which make men ready to sacrifice all, even their lives, for an ideal or for a sentiment. The men who fell upon the decks of the Constitution, or who died at Gettysburg and Shiloh, represent the highest and noblest spirit of which a race is capable. Without that spirit of patriotism, courage, and self-sacrifice no nation can long exist, and the greatest material success in the hands of the cringing and timid will quickly turn to dust and ashes.

The Constitution as she lies in our harbor to-day is an embodiment and memorial of that lofty patriotism. Therefore she should be preserved. Boston has for her a peculiar attachment. Here she was built. Here she was launched. From yonder harbor she went forth to her first and to her last combat, and here she returned scarred with shot, but crowned with her first great victory. We have yet another claim upon her, deeper and stronger still. When she was threatened with destruction fifteen years after the war, she was saved by the lyric verse of a Boston poet, by the "powerful rhyme" which outlasts the gilded monuments of princes. Built, launched, and saved here in Boston, is it any wonder that we have a peculiar attachment to the old frigate and should feel that this ought to be her home and resting-place ?

And yet we know well that she is not our ship. She did not win her victories for Massachusetts, but for the United States. She was the nation's ship and fought the nation's battles beneath the nation's flag. It is the duty, then, of this nation to care for and preserve her. I say duty, because the nation which does not cherish and guard all that stands for the great deeds of the past will have a present and a future barren of aught that posterity will care to recall. With a wise liberality the United States has given three quarters of a million to restore and refit the Hartford, the ship in which Farragut went on to victory, emblem of the sea power which rent the Confederacy in twain, and caught the seaports of the Rebellion in an iron grip. Let the United States give but a third of that sum to restore the Constitution, the last and most famous of the fighting ships which won us place and respect among the nations of the earth.

Turn her into a training vessel, if you will, and let American boys learn from her lessons of patriotism as well as seamanship, but at all events let her be preserved. She represents gallant deeds and goodly victories. She stands for the spirit of patriotism, which uplifts nations and without which no people can be great. So I say all honor to the brave old ship. You may strip her of sails and rigging, cut away her masts and take out her guns, but you never can tear from her the memories which she bears. Let her have, then, now and always the love and honor and care which are hers by right. But whatever befalls, let us at least not suffer her to perish by neglect and fade away from sight like " the dull weed that rots itself in ease at Lethe's Wharf." If we cannot keep her in honor, then let it be said now, even as was said nearly seventy years ago :

"Nail to her mast her holy flag,
Set every threadbare sail,
And give her to the God of storms,
The lightning and the gale."

JOHN MARSHALL [1]

ONE hundred years ago to-day John Marshall was duly sworn in and took his place upon the bench of the Supreme Court as Chief Justice of the United States. There seems to have been no ceremony, no parade, no pomp of any kind about the doing of it. The record of the Supreme Court tells us in dry, official words that on February 4, 1801, the great Virginian lawyer assumed the highest judicial office in the country. That is all. The fact itself dropped so quickly into the babbling current of daily events that the parting of the waters was quite unheard. Yet the circles which this noiseless deed then made in the stream of time have gone on widening with growing force until to-day all over this broad land, everywhere among this mighty nation of nearly eighty millions, the members of a great profession, the teachers and students of universities, the President, the Congress, and the courts, have gathered to commemorate fittingly the official action so quietly performed a century ago. Here, then, it is very plain was a great man, one worthy of much thought

[1] An address delivered before the Bar Associations of Illinois and Chicago at the auditorium in Chicago, February 4, 1901.

and consideration. Is there, indeed, any subject
better worth thought and consideration than a real
man, so great that he not only affected his own time
profoundly, but has projected his influence through
the century, and holds still in a firm grasp the mind
and the imagination of posterity? I am sure that
by thoughtful men this question can be answered
only in the affirmative.

As I have reflected upon that event, so briefly
mentioned in the routine of the Supreme Court
record for the year 1801, there is one thought which
has prevailed in my mind above all others. When
Marshall took the oath as Chief Justice he was
Secretary of State, and for a month he continued to
hold both offices, and to wield very vigorously the
powers of the State Department. Perhaps this may
not strike other minds as of much importance. To
me it seems full of significance. The fact that holding two such offices at the same time is repugnant to
our present ideas of propriety, is in itself worth a
moment's consideration, although it does not contain
the deeper meaning which is to be found in this
incident. It is quite true that to-day no President
would think of permitting the Chief Justice to be a
member of his cabinet for an hour, and no Chief
Justice would allow himself to occupy such a position for an instant. Should such a thing occur, the
storm of adverse criticism which would beat upon

both the President and Chief Justice can be readily imagined. The spectacle of a Chief Justice acting as the chief of a party cabinet and in the spirit of party politics would now shock every one. Then it shocked nobody. In 1801 we were still very near to England in manners and in habits of thought. We had as yet no administrative traditions of our own. Pluralists were not uncommon in English ministries; great judicial officers had often served as ministers of the crown; to this day the highest judicial officer in Great Britain is a member of the cabinet, his place is purely political in tenure, and he rises and falls with his party. The English practice of having the chief law officer a member of the government we have wisely retained in our Attorney-General, but with equal wisdom we have discarded entirely their custom of having judicial officers in high political place. A United States judge to-day can hold no other office, and when he ascends to the bench the door of political preferment closes behind him. All this practice is deeply fixed and rooted now, but it was not so in 1801.

This is not said with any view of defending Marshall. John Adams and the Chief Justice, who remained in his cabinet helping him to fill with tried Federalists every vacant or newly created office, were not only high-minded and honorable men, but absolutely void of offence in this particular. The system

under which they acted is not so good as the one we
have since developed ; that is all. To accuse them of
wrongdoing would be as absurd as the educated
ignorance which, parrot-like, repeats the conventional
cant of its own circle about the decline in the character and standard of our public life at Washington.
If, for example, we are to believe the Maclay Diary,
the first Senate of the United States was corrupt and
decadent to the last degree; the fruit of the Constitution was rotten before it was ripe. But posterity
knows that the first Senate was upright and honorable, composed of able men doing their best — and
their best, although very good, was doubtless imperfect — to solve in hard conflict the difficult problems of
their day. If Maclay was right in picturing the first
Senate as bad, and the professional fault-finder of the
moment is also right in his proposition, that all public
men have declined in character, then we are met
with the startling contradiction that our government
still exists. The trouble is that the contemporary
who can only censure is as untrustworthy as Bache
in his opinion of Washington, or as Greeley and
many others were in their estimate of Lincoln. The
superior person who leads a life of inaction and criticism judges the present by prejudice, and contrasts it
with a past that never existed. From the past, of
which he is ignorant, he eliminates all that is bad,
and from the present, which he does not understand,

he excludes all that is good. It is not to be wondered at that a dark cloud of pessimism broods over his mental landscape, or that he is himself a singularly useless person. In the easy blame which such a critic, arguing in his usual fashion, could throw upon John Marshall for holding political office after he became Chief Justice, there has seemed to me an interesting lesson, so interesting that it has led me into this long digression.

The real meaning of this occupancy of two offices is far different. For a month Marshall was head of the cabinet and head of the judiciary. He was at once statesman and judge, and although he laid down the statesman's place on the 4th of March, 1801, he retained the character to the end of his life, and never ceased to be a statesman while he built up that great reputation which in its breadth and variety surpasses, as I believe, that of any judge or jurist in the splendid legal annals of the English-speaking people.

Many men, far abler and more fit for the task than I, will to-day depict eloquently to the American people the work and the genius of Marshall as lawyer and judge. Upon that inviting field I shall not enter. I shall confine myself to the simpler and humbler task of trying to show how great Marshall was, and how potent his influence has been as a statesman, — a side of his character which, unless my reading has much misled me, has been hitherto neglected, if not overlooked, by eyes dazzled with the brilliancy of his achievements and fame as a lawyer.

But to understand what he was we must, as usual, start with an inquiry. How had he been trained, and what were the qualities which enabled him to play in our history these two great parts as jurist and statesman? He was born one of that small body of people who composed the landowning, slaveholding aristocracy of Virginia at the close of the eighteenth century, and which at that time produced, perhaps, a larger amount of ability in the fields of war, law, and statecraft than any body of equal numbers in modern times and within a similar period. He came of good stock. His mother was a Miss Keith, whose father was cousin-german to the last Earl Marischal of Scotland, and to Frederick's great Field Marshal. His father, whose people appear to have come originally from Wales, was a remarkable man. Planter and pioneer, surveyor and frontiersman, he was a soldier in the old French War, and commanded a Virginia regiment in the war of the Revolution, in which three of his sons also took part. A man of action and of the open air, he nevertheless, despite a narrow fortune, had in his remote home in Fauquier County a good library, and what was still better, a love for books and literature. He had fifteen children and educated them himself, until he brought to his house

a Scotch clergyman named Thompson, the pastor of
the village. In this way the oldest son John studied,
developing a great love for books and for poetry,
while he grew hardy and strong in the outdoor life
and with the rough field sports of a new country.
This lasted until he was fourteen. Then he went to
Westmoreland County, studied with the Rev. Mr.
Campbell, came home to study again with Mr.
Thompson, went as far as Horace and Livy in his
classics, then began to mingle Coke and Blackstone
with his literature, and finally, following his natural
bent, turned entirely to the law. So engaged, the
Revolution found him. More and more, as the noise
of impending strife grew louder, he turned from his
books to drill his company of militiamen. At last
the storm broke, and Lieutenant Marshall, with his
company of riflemen in hunting-shirts, was at the
first fight, when Lord Dunmore was defeated and
driven back to Norfolk. He later joined the Continental Army with his company, was at Brandywine
and Germantown, wintered at Valley Forge, rose to
be a Captain, was brave, popular, and deemed to be
so fair-minded that he was a usual arbiter in all dis-
putes. The next summer he was at Monmouth, when
Washington drove the British finally back into New
York; later he shared in the assault on Stony Point
and in the brilliant enterprise of Paulus Hook.

Soon after this the enlistment term of the men in

Marshall's part of the Virginian line expired, and he went home to stay until the State raised fresh troops. While he waited he attended the lectures on law of Chancellor Wythe, and got a license to practise. Then, weary of inaction, he set out alone and on foot to rejoin the army as a volunteer. Back he came again when his native State was invaded by Leslie in 1780, and fought under Greene and Steuben. He was out again to fight Arnold, and when the would-be seller of West Point had been repulsed, Marshall, still without men to command, resigned his commission in 1781. The war, however, was then practically over, and he had fought all through it.

Now he went to the bar and began to practise in earnest. He met with immediate success and rose with astonishing rapidity. Before he was thirty he was an acknowledged leader at a bar of remarkable ability. With professional work was also mingled much service in the General Assembly, to which he was frequently elected, often greatly against his own wishes. But presently came the convention to consider the Constitution just framed at Philadelphia, and to this Marshall desired and decided to go. Virginia was not friendly to the new scheme; his own county was strongly against it. He was told that if he would promise to oppose the Constitution his return would not be contested. He replied that he wished to go in order to support ratification,

ran, and was elected after a sharp contest in a hostile electorate by sheer force of his personal strength
and popularity. In the convention he played a
great part. He contended successfully with Patrick
Henry, and if he had not the glowing eloquence of
the elder man, there was none stronger than he in
reasoning, more unanswerable, more convincing. He
was one of the determined leaders who finally wrung
from an unfriendly convention an unwilling majority
of ten votes in favor of the Constitution.

Back he went to his courts and his cases. He had
gone to the convention, not for political preferment,
but to get the Constitution ratified, and the victory
was all he wanted. Still he could not escape service
in the Assembly, and as Washington's administration
developed its policies, and Virginia, under the delicate manipulation of Jefferson, turned more and
more against her great President, Marshall fought the
battles of his old chief in the Legislature, and on one
occasion, at least, carried a vote of confidence in the
National Government. Thus without thought and
in his own despite he became conspicuous beyond
the borders of Virginia. Public men in other States
began to look with interest and admiration upon the
lawyer already distinguished at the bar who, with
perfect courage and great intellectual power, was
fighting the battle of Washington in an anti-Federal-
ist community; a man who did not fear even to de-

fend in Virginia the Jay treaty in the darkest hour
of its unpopularity.   Marshall himself in one of his
rare letters speaks of the warm manner in which the
leading New England Federalists received him in
Philadelphia, filled with wonder that a man so sound
in opinion should exist in Virginia.

With a political reputation growing and expanding
so fast, it was only a question of time when he would
be called to do national work.   Washington desired
that he should accept the mission to France, but he
declined.   Later the same offer came from President
Adams, and this time the circumstances were such that
Marshall felt it to be his duty to accept.   Our relations with France had gone from bad to worse.   The
French government had treated us as if we were little
else than a vassal state.   They had seized our ships
and spared us no insult.   The spirit of the country
was rising, and the dominant Federalists, if not
eager, were certainly not averse to a war with the
revolutionary government at Paris, with which their
political opponents sympathized and which seemed to
them representative of those forces of anarchy and
disorder which it was their own especial mission on
earth to combat.   Mr. Adams, however, feeling profoundly, as Washington had felt in the case of England, the peril of war to our new government, was
determined to exhaust every effort to preserve peace
with our former ally, although the France of the

revolution was as distasteful to him as to any of the Federalist leaders. With this purpose in view he joined John Marshall and Elbridge Gerry with Charles Cotesworth Pinckney, who had been refused recognition as Minister, in a special mission of peace to settle the differences between the two countries. This was the duty which Marshall felt he could not refuse, and he accordingly sailed from Philadelphia for Amsterdam on the 17th of July, 1797.

Into the history of that famous mission it is not necessary to enter. The course of the Directory and of Talleyrand was in all ways characteristic of one of the most corrupt governments of modern times. Our envoys were flouted, refused recognition or reception, and were informed by base but accurate agents that their only way to obtain their object was to bribe, first, Talleyrand, then the Directory, and then France herself. The American envoys, like honest men, rejected all these advances absolutely and with ill-concealed disgust. The American case, stated in an argument of great ability, drawn by John Marshall, was also laid before Talleyrand. But that eminent person was not interested in arguments. What he wanted was money. Pinckney and Marshall saw this clearly enough, secured their passports, not, it may be added, without incurring plenty of fresh insults, and took their departure. Gerry, deluded and hoodwinked by Talleyrand, remained, and when a new commission was sent peace was made, not because Gerry stayed or because John Adams broke with his party in renewing his efforts for peaceful settlement, but because hostilities had begun, and Truxtun's guns and shattered French frigates had taught France that if we would not bribe we could at least fight. When Marshall returned to America he found events had moved rapidly toward the fighting stage. The letters inviting our envoys to bribery and corruption as well as to humiliation had been published, and the country was filled with righteous wrath. Marshall was received with acclaim as loud as it was deserved, and it was at a banquet in his honor that the words attributed to Pinckney were given as a toast: "Millions for defence, but not one cent for tribute." This was the sentiment of the country as well as of the dinner-table, and it portended a severe reaction against the party of France so ably led by Jefferson.

Into that party struggle Marshall had no intention of entering. He had performed well and fearlessly a duty which he had not sought, and his one wish now was to go back to his office and his clients and to the profession which he loved. But it was not to be. President Adams offered him a seat on the Supreme Court Bench, which he declined, but refusal was not so easy when he was summoned to Mount Vernon and urged to stand for Congress.

The course of Jefferson and the anti-Federalists with
their French sympathies had alarmed Washington
profoundly.   He felt that in order to sustain the
government the Federalist party must be supported.
He had led that party in his last years of office, and
he was so impressed by the political perils of the
time and by the growing power of foreign influence
that he could not remain inactive now.   So Marshall
listened to the voice which seldom spoke in vain to
any American a century ago, and much against his
will became a candidate for Congress.   His honest
and manly stand in Paris and the honor and applause he had gained at home, however, could not
save him from the attacks of Jefferson and his followers.   They opposed him strenuously, crying out
against him as a monarchist, which was the Jeffer-
sonian language to describe any man who liked a
strong central government or who believed that the
United States was a nation and not an alliance of
petty republics.   The contest was heated and the
majority small, but Marshall won, and aided by his
personal popularity carried the Richmond district, —
a very considerable feat.

The Congress to which he was chosen was a memorable one.   The Federalist party by sheer force of
ability, not only in the Executive but in both
branches of Congress, had established the new
government, organized its machinery, and founded

its policies. It was a vitally necessary work, but
the men who had wrought it had not only incurred
the usual hostility which always meets those who
are doers of deeds, but they also had the additional
unpopularity which was due both to their superior
abilities and their uncompromising and often over-
bearing methods. They had carried their measures
with difficulty, for they rarely possessed a working
majority in Congress, and this condition had been a
useful check upon them. Now, however, the attempt
of France to bribe our envoys had produced a just re-
vulsion of feeling against the party of Jefferson,
which had made extravagant admiration of France
a test of American patriotism, and in the true colonial
spirit forced our politics to turn upon the affairs
of Europe. The Federalists carried the election
triumphantly, and found themselves with a majority
such as they had never known. Successful and
effective under difficult and adverse conditions,
unlimited power turned their heads, and their over-
bearing and arrogant tendencies asserted themselves.
Their victory became the precursor of their ruin.

John Marshall, living in a hostile atmosphere, a
Federalist in Virginia, was a party man of the hard
fibre which is found under such circumstances, but
he also had learned in the same school to gauge
public opinion and the possibilities of action far
better than the men of the North, accustomed to

Federalist supremacy. Extreme men from New England thought him over-moderate, if not wavering, because he voted against those natural but most injudicious measures, the Alien and Sedition Acts. In doing so Marshall was neither timid nor wavering, but simply wise, as the events of the next four years were to show. And if his critics could have looked afar into the future they would have seen the Virginian Federalist, whose beliefs were founded upon a rock, alone and in the midst of enemies upholding and extending the principles they loved, when many of their own faith had deserted or fallen by the wayside, after their party organization had disappeared, and even when their great party name had passed out of existence and was heard only as a byword and a reproach.

But whether thought too moderate in his views or not, John Marshall went to the front as a leader of his party and as a leader of the House. He shrank from no conflict, and upheld the fundamental principles of his party in a manner of which few men were capable. The conspicuous triumph of his congressional career, and space forbids the mention of any other, was his argument in the Jonathan Robbins case. Thomas Nash, alias Jonathan Robbins, taking part in a mutiny, had committed a murder on a British frigate, escaped, been captured in this country, and then resisted extradition on the ground that he was an American who had been impressed. President Adams directed that he should be given up if his identity were proved as well as grounds sufficient for commitment had the crime been committed in the United States. The court thought both facts were proved, and the man, who later confessed that he was not an American, was given up by the President's order under a clause of the Jay treaty. It is quite needless to explain that an administration which undertakes to respect and fulfil treaty obligations to England is an inviting object of attack to the thinkers of the opposing party, and presents a tempting field for the investment of political capital. Mr. Livingston of New York introduced a resolution censuring the President for his action, more especially for his interference with the judiciary, and Marshall spoke for the defence. Into that luminous and convincing argument I cannot enter here. Albert Gallatin sat near the speaker taking notes for a reply. The pencil moved more and more slowly, the notes became fewer and fewer, and at last stopped. " Do you not mean to reply to him ? " said a friend. " I do not," said Gallatin, " because I cannot." Many of the opposition thought the same, and the resolution was defeated by a vote of nearly two to one.

Marshall's career in the House, however, was as

short as it was brilliant. The break had finally come
between Mr. Adams and the Hamiltonian Federalists
in his cabinet whom he had inherited from Washington. Wherever the right lay it was a lamentable
business, and a potent cause of the Federalist defeat.
The remoter consequences of this famous quarrel do
not concern us here, but the immediate result was
the retirement of McHenry from the War Department, which was at once offered to Marshall and
declined. Hard upon McHenry's withdrawal came
that of Pickering from the Department of State, and
this great post Marshall accepted, resigning his seat in
Congress in order to do so. It was a difficult and
thankless task to assume these duties just at the close
of an administration, with defeat impending and the
party divided into bitterly hostile factions. Yet
such was Marshall's tact and such the respect for his
character that he commanded the confidence of the
whole party. He completely satisfied Mr. Adams
and yet retained the intimate friendship of Hamilton. He was entirely true to the President's policy
and yet held the admiring regard of Wolcott, and
even of Pickering, whom he supplanted. In the
foreign relations with which he was charged the time
was too short for the full development of his influence, but we can see in his despatches the strong
American spirit and the quiet but unflinching way
in which he gave other nations to understand that

we must go along our own paths, and that our dealings with one nation were no rightful concern of any other.

The last troubled months of the Adams administration, however, soon came to an end. On the 4th of March, 1801, a month after he had been sworn in as Chief Justice, Marshall retired from the State Department. Let us look at him a moment as he stands at the threshold of his great career. He is forty-five years old and in the full maturity of his powers. He is very tall, very spare, rather loose-jointed and careless in his movements. A little ungainly, perhaps, one observer thinks, with the air of the mountains and of the early outdoor life still about him. Evidently muscular and strong; temperate, too, with all the vigor of health and constitution which any work or responsibility may demand. He is not handsome of face with his angular features and thick, unruly hair growing low on his forehead over rather small but very piercing black eyes. None the less the face is full of intelligence and force, and all observers, however much they differ in details, alike agree that the bright eyes are full of fun, and that about the firm-set mouth there plays a smile which tells of that generous and hearty sense of humor which pierces sham and, as Story says, is too honest for intrigue.

No one can say to-day whether Marshall realized

as he left the State Department that the great work
of his life lay all before him. We know it now, — know
that all his past career had been only preparatory for
that which was to come. And what a training it
had been! First of all, he was a lawyer, made so by
the strong bent of his mind, in the full tide of successful practice, and holding his well-won place in
the front rank of the American bar. He had been
a soldier of long and hard service, and had faced
death in battle many times. A wide parliamentary
experience had been his, drawn from many terms in
the Virginia Legislature, from the Constitutional Convention, and a session of Congress. He had been in
Europe, had seen European politics at close range,
and had measured swords with the ablest, most un-
scrupulous, and most corrupt statesman and diplomatist of the Old World. He had served as a
Cabinet Minister, and there had studied the relations
of his country to the movements of world politics.
He had been a man of affairs great and small, and
had lived and fought in the world of men. This
varied education, these diverse experiences, may
seem to have been superfluous for one who was to
fill a purely judicial office, and yet they were never
more valuable to any man than to him who was to
be the Chief Justice of the United States at that precise period. When Marshall laid down the statesman's office and took up that of the lawyer, his work

as a statesman was still to do. How great that work was I shall try to show.

When Marshall took his seat on the Supreme Bench, he brought with him not only his legal genius and training and his wide and various experience in politics and diplomacy, but also certain fixed convictions. He was a man who formed opinions slowly, and who did not indulge himself in a large collection of cardinal principles. But the opinions which he formed and the principles which he adopted after much hard and silent thought were immovable, and by them he steered, for they were as constant as the stars. He had one of those rare minds which never confound the passing with the eternal or mix the accidental and trivial with the things vital and necessary. Hence the compatibility between his absolute fixity of purpose in certain well-ascertained directions and his wise moderation and large tolerance as to all else. To these qualities was joined another even rarer, the power of knowing what the essential principle was. In every controversy and in every argument he went unerringly to the heart of the question, for he had that mental quality which Dr. Holmes compared to the instinct of the tiger for the jugular vein. As he plucked out the heart of a law case or a debate in Congress, so he seized on the question which overrode all others in the politics of the United States and upon which all else turned.

This vital question was whether the United States should be a nation, or a confederacy of jarring and petty republics, destined to strife, disintegration, and decay. In a well-known letter to a friend, Marshall says that he entered the Revolution filled with " wild and enthusiastic notions." Most young men of that period, imbued with such ideas, remained under their control, and in the course of events became ardent sympathizers with the unbridled fanaticisms of the French Revolution, or at least ardent opponents of anything like a strong and well-ordered government, and equally zealous supporters of State rights and separatist doctrines. Not so John Marshall. With characteristic modesty he ascribes the fact that he did not continue under the dominion of his " wild and enthusiastic notions" to accident and circumstances when it really was due to his own clear and powerful intellect. In the struggle with England he came to see that the only hope of victory lay in devotion to a common cause, in being soldiers of the Union and not of separate colonies, and that the peril was in the weakness of the general government. It seems simple enough to say this now, but the central idea was as a rule grasped feebly and imperfectly, if at all, by the young men of that period. Like Hamilton, Marshall worked it out for himself; and in that same letter he says that it was during the war that he came to regard America as his country and Congress

as his government. From that time he was an
American first and a Virginian second, and from the
convictions thus formed in camp and on the march
he never swerved. Here was the ruling principle
of his public life, and to the establishment of that
principle his whole career and all his great powers
were devoted. This made him a Federalist. It was
this very devotion to a fundamental principle which
was the source of that temperate wisdom which
made him avoid the Alien and Sedition Acts, because
by their violence they endangered the success of the
party which had in charge something too precious to
be risked by indulging even the just passion of the
moment. But the moderation in what he regarded
as non-essential was accompanied by an absolutely
unyielding attitude when the vital question was
touched. Despite the criticisms of the extreme
Federalists upon his liberality, there was no more
rigid believer in the principles which had brought
that party into existence than the man who became
Chief Justice one hundred years ago.

Holding these beliefs, what was there for him to
do, what could he do in a position wholly judicial
and with every other branch of the government in
the hands of his political foes? He was confined to a
strictly limited province. To his political opponents
the entire field of political action was open. At the
head of these opponents was Thomas Jefferson, who

hated him intensely. It could not well be otherwise. Not only were these two Virginians politically opposed, but they were antagonistic in nature and temperament. "There are some men," said Rufus Choate, "whom we hate for cause, and others whom we hate peremptorily." Both descriptions apply to the feeling which Jefferson cherished toward Marshall. They were as wide apart as the poles. Jefferson wrote brave, blustering words about the desirability of "watering the tree of liberty once in twenty years with the blood of tyrants," and was himself the most peaceful of men, one who shrank from war and recoiled from bloodshed, and who was a rather grotesque figure of a war governor in hurried flight when the British invaded Virginia. Marshall had served in the army for five years. The hunger and cold of Valley Forge, the trials of the march, the dangers of retreat, the perils of many battles, the grim hazards of the night assault, were all familiar to him, and he never talked at all about watering anything with blood or about bloodshed of any sort. Jefferson was timid in action; subtle, acute, and brilliant in intellect, given to creeping methods. To him, therefore, Marshall, the man of powerful mind, who was as simple and direct as he was absolutely fearless, and who marched straight to his object with his head up and his eyes on his foe, was particularly obnoxious. Marshall, moreover, had crossed Jefferson in many ways. He

had led opposition to him in Virginia, and had
wrested from him a Congressional district. Now
Marshall was placed in a great position, beyond the
reach of assault, and yet where he could observe,
and perhaps thwart, Jefferson's most cherished
schemes. Marshall in his own way entirely recipro-
cated Jefferson's feelings. He distrusted him and
despised his methods, his foreign prejudices, and,
what seemed to Marshall, his devious ways. So
strong was this hostility that it almost led him to
make what would have been the one political mistake of his life, by supporting Burr for the Presidency when the election of 1800 was thrown into
the House of Representatives. From this he was
saved by his own wisdom and good sense, which
were convinced, by Hamilton's reasoning, that Jefferson, whom Marshall knew, was a less evil than Burr,
whom he did not know, but who was known only
too well to Hamilton.[1]

[1] He wrote of Jefferson to Hamilton in 1801 that " by weakening
the office of President he will increase his personal power. He will
diminish his reponsibility, sap the fundamental principles of the
government, and become the leader of that party which is about to
constitute the majority in the legislature. The morals of the author
of the letter to Mazzei cannot be pure."

Van Santvoord says, in his "Lives of the Chief Justices," p. 342,
on the authority of an eyewitness, that after Burr's trial there was
a final cessation of all personal intercourse between Jefferson and
Marshall, and that two or three of the Justices of the Supreme Court
followed the example of their chief.

Age did not change or soften Marshall's opinion of Jefferson. In

Jefferson and his party came into power with a great predominance destined to grow more complete

1821 (July 13) he wrote to Judge Story (Proceedings Massachusetts Historical Society for October and November, 1900, p. 328):

" What you say of Mr. Jefferson's letter rather grieves than surprises me.* It grieves me because his influence is still so great that many, very many, will adopt his opinions, however unsound they may be, and however contradictory to their own reason. I cannot describe the surprise and mortification I have felt at hearing that Mr. Madison has embraced them with respect to the judicial department.

" For Mr. Jefferson's opinion as respects this department it is not difficult to assign the cause. He is among the most ambitious, and, I suspect, among the most unforgiving of men. His great power is over the mass of the people, and this power is chiefly acquired by professions of democracy. Every check on the wild impulse of the moment is a check on his own power, and he is unfriendly to the source from which it flows. He looks, of course, with ill will at an independent judiciary.

" That in a free country with a written constitution any intelligent man should wish a dependent judiciary, or should think that the Constitution is not a law for the court as well as the legislature, would astonish me, if I had not learnt from observation that with many men the judgment is completely controlled by the passions. The case of the mandamus may be the cloak, but the Batture † is recollected with still more resentment."

Again he wrote on September 18, 1821:

" A deep design to convert our government into a mere league of States has taken strong hold of a powerful and violent party in Virginia. The attack upon the judiciary is in fact an attack upon the Union. The judicial department is well understood to be that through which the government may be attacked most successfully, because it is without patronage, and of course without power. And it is equally well understood that every subtraction from its jurisdiction is a vital wound to the government itself. The attack upon it

---

* The letter here commented on was probably the letter to William C. Jarvis, printed in Washington's edition of the Writings of Thomas Jefferson, vol. 7, pp. 177–179, in which Jefferson denies the right of the Judges to issue a mandamus to any "executive or legislative officer to enforce the fulfilment of their official duties," and asserts that it is a "very dangerous doctrine" to "consider the judges as the ultimate arbiters of all constitutional questions."

† The first of these references is to the opinion of the Chief Justice in the case of Marbury v. Madison (1 Cranch, 153). The second reference is to the protracted litigation which involved the title to what was known as the Batture, near New Orleans, and in which Mr. Jefferson took a strong personal interest.

as the years went by.   They were in principle
hostile to the government which they were chosen
to conduct.   They were flushed with victory.   They
meant to sweep away all the Federalists had done;

therefore is a masked battery aimed at the government itself.   The
whole attack, if not originating with Mr. Jefferson, is obviously
approved and guided by him.   It is therefore formidable in other
States as well as in this, and it behooves the friends of the Union to
be more on the alert than they have been.   An effort will certainly
be made to repeal the twenty-fifth section of the judicial act."

In December, 1832, he wrote to Judge Story about the nullification
resolutions of South Carolina, then under discussion in Virginia.
The following passage is of great interest as showing his profound
comprehension of the movement coupled with his accurate prediction
of the fate of West Virginia, which came to pass thirty years later,
as well as his undying feeling against Jefferson as the originator of
these evils:

" On Thursday these resolutions are to be taken up, and the debate
will, I doubt not, be ardent and tempestuous enough.   I pretend not
to anticipate the result.   Should it countenance the obvious design of
South Carolina to form a Southern Confederacy, it may conduce to a
southern league — never to a Southern government.   Our theories are
incompatible with a government for more than a single State.   We
can form no union which shall be closer than an alliance between
sovereigns.   In this event there is some reason to apprehend internal
convulsion.   The northern and western section of our State, should
a union be maintained north of the Potomac, will not readily connect
itself with the South.   At least, such is the present belief of their
most intelligent men.   Any effort on their part to separate from
Southern Virginia and unite with a Northern Confederacy may probably be punished as treason.   ' We have fallen on evil times.'"
" I thank you for Mr. Webster's speech.   Entertaining the opinion
he has expressed respecting the general course of the administration,
his patriotism is entitled to the more credit for the determination he
expressed at Faneuil Hall to support it in the great effort it promises
to make for the preservation of the Union.   No member of the then
opposition avowed a similar determination during the Western Insur-
rection, which would have been equally fatal had it not been quelled
by the well-timed vigor of General Washington.   We are now gathering the bitter fruits of the tree even before that time planted by
Mr. Jefferson, and so industriously and perseveringly cultivated by
Virginia."

they intended to interpret the Constitution until
naught was left and put the national government
and the national life into a strait-jacket. In the
process of time they found themselves helpless in
the grip of circumstances and governing by the
system of Washington and Hamilton, whose methods
and organization were too strong for them to overthrow. But at the start this was not apparent.
The separatist principle seemed to be supreme, and
Jefferson's followers threw themselves upon the work
of the Federalists, and in their rage even undertook
to break down the judiciary by the process of im-
peachment, — a scheme which failed miserably, but
which no doubt cherished the hope of reaching at
last to the chief of all the Judges.

In their pleasant plans and anticipations of revenge it must have seemed as if nothing could stop
the onset of an all-powerful President backed by
a subservient Congress. Surely the national principle, the national life, the broad construction of the
Constitution, would shrivel away before such an
attack. There seemed no one in the way, for however much Jefferson, ever watchful, may have suspected, his own followers certainly did not reckon
as very formidable the great lawyer sitting far apart
in the cold seclusion of a court room. Yet there
the enemy was. There he sat intrenched. His
powers were limited, but his opponents were to find

out what he could do with them. They were to
learn by bitter experiences that even these limited
powers in the hands of a great man were sufficient
to extend the Constitution and to build it up faster
and far more surely than they by Executive act or
Congressional speeches could narrow it or pull it
down. Those of them who survived were destined
to behold the ark of the national life, carried through
the dark years of the first decade of the century,
emerge in safety ere the second closed, and the
national principle which they had sought to smother
rise up in great assertion and with a more splendid
vitality than any one dreamed possible as the fourth
decade began and the man who had done the deed sank
into his grave in all the majesty of his eighty years.

How did John Marshall do this work, this statesman's work as Chief Justice of the United States?
It is all there in his decisions. To show it forth as
it deserves would require a volume. Only an outline which will roughly mark out the highest peaks
in the range is possible here.

The first blow was struck in 1803, in the famous
case of Marbury against Madison. Marbury applied
for a mandamus to compel Mr. Madison to deliver
to him his commission as justice of the peace, which
had been signed and sealed by Mr. Adams and
withheld by his successor. Marshall held that the
applicant had a right to the commission; that his

right having been violated, the law of the country
afforded a remedy; that the case in its nature
was one for mandamus, but that being an original
process, the Supreme Court had no jurisdiction, because the act of Congress conferring such jurisdiction, not being authorized by the Constitution, was
null and void. He declared, in other words, that
the Constitution was supreme, that any law of Congress in conflict with it was null and void, that the
Supreme Court was to decide whether this conflict
existed; and then, going beyond the point involved,
he boldly announced that if the application had been
properly made, the Federal court could compel the
Executive to perform a certain act. At one stroke
he lifted the National Constitution to the height
of authority, and made the tremendous assertion of
power in the court, which he declared could nullify
the action of Congress and control that of the Executive if the necessary conditions should arise.
Small wonder is it that Jefferson was irritated and
alarmed to the last degree, and that he complained
bitterly of the manner in which the Chief Justice
had travelled out of the record in order to tell the
world that he might, if he so willed, curb the authority of the President. But the assertion of the
supremacy of the Constitution and of the power
of the court to decide a law unconstitutional has
remained unshaken from that day to this.

In Marbury against Madison, Marshall asserted the supremacy of the Constitution and the power of the court in relation to the other branches of the National Government. But important and far reaching as this was, the vital struggle was not among the departments created by the same instrument. The conflict upon which the fate of the country turned was between the forces of union and the forces of separation, between the power of the nation and the rights of the States. It was here that Marshall did his greatest work, and it was this issue which he desired to meet above all others.

In the case of the United States against Peters in 1809, he decided that a State could not annul the judgment, or determine the jurisdiction, or destroy rights, acquired under the judgments of the courts of the United States. Thus he set the national courts above the States, and he followed this up in the following year by deciding, in Fletcher against Peck, that a grant of lands was a contract within the meaning of the Constitution, and that a State law annulling such a grant was in conflict with the Constitution of the United States, and therefore null and void. The United States courts, it was to be henceforth understood, were not only above and beyond the reach of State legislatures, but they could nullify the laws of such legislatures. No heavier or better directed blow was ever struck against State rights when those rights were invoked in order to thwart or cripple the national power.

The trial of Burr in 1807, although not bearing upon the central principles to which Marshall devoted his best efforts, gave him an opportunity to define treason under the Constitution. On this memorable trial there can be no doubt that he stood between the accused, whom the government wished to destroy, and the just popular sentiment which would have fain hurried Burr to the gallows. That Marshall's rulings were correct and that he laid down the American law and definition of treason in a manner which subsequent generations have accepted, cannot be questioned. But this cannot be said of the famous ruling by which he granted the motion to issue a *subpœna duces tecum*, directed to the President of the United States. If his desire was to fill Jefferson with impotent anger and with a sense of affront and humiliation, he succeeded amply. In any other view granting the motion was a failure and a mistake, for instead of exhibiting the power of the court it showed its limitations. The Chief Executive of the nation clearly cannot be brought to court against his will, for higher duties are imposed upon him, and still more decisive is the practical consideration that the court is physically powerless to enforce its decrees against the Chief Magistrate, by whom alone in the last resort the decrees of the court can be carried into execution. The animosity toward Jefferson which nearly led Marshall into the political blunder of supporting Burr in 1801 was the probable cause of this single mistake in his long management of the judicial power. Yet even though it was an error, it gives a vivid idea of the bold spirit which was able to make a limited court not only the bulwark of the Constitution, but the chief engine in advancing national principles during a long series of years, when every other department was arrayed against it and a hostile political party was everywhere predominant.

To assert the supremacy of the National Constitution over the constitutions and laws of the States was, however, only half the battle, and was in its nature a defensive position. It was necessary not only to maintain but to advance. It was not enough for the Constitution to stand firm; it must be made to march, and this was done by a series of great decisions, through which Marshall developed and extended the constitutional powers and authority, not merely of his own court, but of the Executive and of Congress. In 1805, in the United States against Fisher, he found in the clause of the Constitution giving Congress the right to pass all necessary and proper laws for carrying into execution the powers vested in them by the Constitution, authority for a law making the United States a preferred creditor. In 1819, the Dartmouth College Case, the most famous perhaps of all Marshall's cases, was decided. In this he gave to the clause relating to the impairment of contracts, already used as the foundation of the judgment in the case of Fletcher against Peck, a vigorous reinforcement and extension. In holding that a State could not alter a charter derived from the British Crown in colonial times, the Chief Justice carried the constitutional power in this regard to an extreme, justifiable, no doubt, but from which a man less bold would have recoiled.

In the same year he pushed the same doctrine home in Sturges against Crowninshield, holding that a State could not pass an insolvent law releasing debts contracted before its passage.

In the still greater case of McCullough against Maryland, also heard at this time, he affirmed and extended the national power with one hand while he struck down the authority of the State with the other. No man could add much to the argument in which Hamilton defended the constitutionality of a National Bank, but Marshall presented it again in a manner equal to that of the great Secretary, and which carried with it an authority which only the court could give. He held the bank to be constitutional under " the necessary laws " clause, and in one of those compact, nervous sentences, so charac-

teristic of the man, he defined once for all the scope
of that provision. " Let this end be legitimate," he
said, " let it be within the scope of the Constitution,
and all means which are appropriate, which are
plainly adapted to that end, which are not prohibited, but consist with the letter and spirit of the
Constitution, are constitutional." What an enlargement of national power is contained in these
pregnant words! What a weapon did this single
weighty sentence place in the national armory!
The constitutionality of the bank being thus affirmed, the law of Maryland taxing its branches
fell, of course, as null and void, for the power to tax
is the power to destroy.

That profound legal thinker, Andrew Jackson,
differed from Marshall on this question.   He
wrecked the bank of the United States, fostered the
pet State banks, and left the panic of 1837 to desolate business, and overwhelm his successor and his
party in defeat.   But although Jackson tore down
the superstructure, upon the foundation laid by Marshall in an opinion, where the foresight of the statesman went hand in hand with the matchless reasoning
of the lawyer, arose the national bank system, which,
after forty years, still stands before us unshaken
and secure.

Two years after the Maryland case, in Cohens
against Virginia, he held that the appellate jurisdic-

tion of the Supreme Court extended to decisions of
the highest State courts, and that a State itself could
be brought into court when the validity of the State
law under the National Constitution was involved.

In 1824, in Gibbons against Ogden, he interpreted
and breathed life into the clause giving Congress
power to regulate commerce, and held unconstitutional a law of the State of New York which was in
conflict with that clause. In so doing he overruled
some of the ablest judges of the State of New York,
and cut off a right hitherto supposed to be unquestioned. But he did not hesitate, and another
extension of the national power followed.

In Craig and others against the State of Missouri,
under the clause forbidding a State to emit bills of
credit, he annulled a law of that State which authorized the issue of loan certificates which were held to
come within the prohibited description.

In The Cherokee Nation against Georgia, he held
that the Indians were not a foreign nation, and
therefore not entitled to sue in the Supreme Court ;
and then, with his wonted felicity of phrase, he described them as a " domestic and dependent " nation
dwelling within the boundaries of the United States
and subject only to the laws and treaties of the
central government — a proposition capable of wide
application, and carrying with it possibilities of a
great extension of the national authority. Follow-

ing out this principle in the case of Worcester against Georgia, he held that a citizen of the United States going into the Cherokee country could not be held amenable to the laws of Georgia. The administration was out of sympathy with Marshall's views, the State of Georgia was openly defiant, yet after some months of delay the State gave way, the missionaries were released, and the court triumphed.

In this list of cases, so baldly stated, many have been omitted and none has been explained and analyzed as it deserves. But these examples, chosen from among the greatest and most familiar, serve to show the course which Marshall pursued through thirty-five years of judicial life. These decisions are more than a monument of legal reasoning, more than a masterly exposition of the Constitution, for they embody the well-considered policy of a great statesman. They are the work of a man who saw that the future of the United States hinged upon the one question whether the national should prevail over the separatist principle, whether the nation was to be predominant over the States — whether, indeed, there was to be a nation at all. Through all the issues which rose and fell during these thirty-five years, through all the excitements of the passing day, through Louisiana acquisitions and the relations with France and England, through embargoes and war and Missouri Compromises, and all the bitter absorbing passions which they aroused, the Chief Justice in his court went steadily forward dealing with that one underlying question beside which all others were insignificant. Slowly but surely he did his work. He made men understand that a tribunal existed before which States could be forced to plead, by which State laws could be annulled, and which was created by the Constitution. He took the dry clauses of that Constitution and breathed into them the breath of life. Knowing well the instinct of human nature to magnify its own possessions — an instinct more potent than party feeling — he had pointed out and developed for Presidents and Congresses the powers given them by the Constitution from which they derived their own existence. Whether these Presidents and Congresses were Federalist or Democratic, they were all human and would be certain, therefore, to use sooner or later the powers disclosed to them. That which Hamilton in the bitterness of defeat had called " a frail and worthless fabric," Marshall converted into a mighty instrument of government. The Constitution which began as an agreement between conflicting States, Marshall, continuing the work of Washington and Hamilton, transformed into a charter of national life. When his own life closed his work was done — a nation had been made. Before he died he heard this great fact declared with unrivalled eloquence by Webster, although the attitude of the South at that moment filled him with gloomy apprehensions and made him fear that the Constitution had failed.[1] It was reserved to another generation to put Marshall's work to the last and awful test of war and to behold it come forth from that dark ordeal, triumphant and supreme.

What of the man who did all this? The statesman we know, the great lawyer, the profound jurist, the original thinker, the unrivalled reasoner. All this is there in his decisions and in his public life, carved deep in the history of the times. But of the man himself we know little; in proportion to his greatness and the part he played we know almost nothing. He was a silent man, doing his great work in the world and saying nothing of himself, to a degree quite unknown to any of the heroes of Carlyle, who preached the doctrine of silence so strenuously in many volumes. Marshall seems to have destroyed all his own papers; certainly none of consequence are known to exist now. He wrote but few letters, if we may judge from the voluminous collections of the time, where, if we except those addressed to Judge Story, lately published, he is less represented than any of the other leaders of

[1] See Letters to Story, Proceedings of Massachusetts Historical Society for October, 1900.

that period. Brief memoirs by some of his contemporaries, scattered letters, stray recollections and fugitive descriptions, are all that we have to help us to see and know the man John Marshall. Yet his personality is so strong that from these fragments and from the study of his public life it stands forth to all who look with understanding and sympathy. A great intellect; a clear sight which was never dimmed, but which always recognized facts and scorned delusions ; a powerful will ; a courage, moral, mental, and physical, which nothing could daunt, — all these things lie upon the surface. Deeper down we discern a directness of mind, a purity and strength of character, a kind heart, an abundant humor, and a simplicity and modesty which move our admiration as beyond the bounds of eulogy. He was a very great man. The proofs of his greatness lie all about us, in our history, our law, our constitutional development, our public thought. But there is one witness to his greatness of soul which seems to me to outweigh all the others. He had been soldier and lawyer and statesman ; he had been an envoy to France, a member of Congress, Secretary of State, and Chief Justice. He did a great work, and no one knew better than he how great it had been. Then when he came to die he wrote his own epitaph, and all he asked to have recorded was his name, the date of his birth, the date of his marriage, and the date of his death. What a noble pride and what a fine simplicity are there ! In the presence of such a spirit, at the close of such a life, almost anything that can be said would seem tawdry and unworthy. His devoted friend, Judge Story, wished to have inscribed upon Marshall's tomb the words " Expounder of the Constitution." Even this is something too much and also far too little. He is one of that small group of men who have founded States. He is a Nation-maker, a State-builder. His monument is in the history of the United States, and his name is written upon the Constitution of his country.

OLIVER ELLSWORTH [1]

In this presence and on an occasion like this
tradition and custom alike suggest that I should
speak to you either of the law, of the part which
those who follow that honored profession have taken
in our history, or of that which they ought now to
take in the life of our time. Yet, rash as it may
seem, in addressing those whose studies have taught
them more than any other studies can teach the importance of precedents, I shall do neither. I shall
not speak to you of laws or constitutions, but of a
maker of both. I shall not try to discourse to you
upon the place which the legal profession has filled
in the past, or that which it ought to fill in society
and politics to-day, but I shall ask your attention to
what one lawyer achieved during a most momentous
period of our history. I shall not, as the common
phrase has it, descend from the general to the particular, but I shall advance from the boundless
region of abstract principles to the sharply defined
facts of a great example. I propose to speak to you
of a man who in his time played many parts, who

[1] An address delivered at New Haven before the graduating class
of the Law School of Yale University, June 23, 1902.

was a State judge, and Chief Justice of the United States, a framer of the Constitution, a maker of laws when the Federal Statute Book offered a blank page, a statesman, a Senator, a diplomatist. Here, indeed, is an impressive list of public positions of the highest rank; but public office is, after all, only an opportunity, and there is many a case where all has been said of the holder when the places he held have been duly catalogued. That which concerns posterity is what the man did with his opportunity, what he meant to his own generation, what he means to us.

To me, Oliver Ellsworth, who filled the spacious places and met the large opportunities which I have enumerated, has come to mean a good deal. Historians, students, and lawyers know Oliver Ellsworth, not intimately perhaps, but still they have an acquaintance with him sufficient to give a certain reality to his name. Yet my own recent inquiries have led me to fear that to most of us he is little more than a name, that he has dropped most undeservedly into that interesting but rather pathetic group of historic figures to whom Froude gave the melancholy title of " Forgotten Worthies." He has richly merited a better fate, and should find a biographer with room and verge enough to do him full justice. But while we await the biographer, if we cannot build a fitting monument, we can at least add something to the cairn which history in its progress has already gathered to preserve his memory.

Let us try first to place him aright. He was not one of the greatest leaders of an extraordinary period. He cannot stand with the man who was dominant in that period alike in peace and war, our first President. He had not the creative power and fiery force of Hamilton nor the profound originality and sweeping conceptions of John Marshall. But he was one of that remarkable body of men who gathered round these leaders of war, statecraft, and politics, and without whom the leaders could not have succeeded. Oliver Ellsworth was a fine example of a fine type. The contribution to human history at that time and in this country, made by the men whom he exemplified, was expressed in the campaigns and government of Washington, in the policies and organizations of Hamilton, and in the decisions of Marshall. It consists of the American Revolution and the formation of the United States. Follow our own history from that day to this, consider what the United States is to the world at the present time, and you can see how momentous and how far reaching was the work of those men who tore one empire asunder and then laid firm and deep the foundations of another. If you seek their monument, " Survey mankind from China to Peru," and when your eyes rest at last upon the United States you will have found it.

All actors, great and small alike, in the decisive crises of history, when the world turns in her sleep with pain and wakes to give birth, after much sore travail, to vast changes in the relations of men and in the movements of society, have a deep meaning. Every man, for example, who stands out in relief against the red light of the French Terror has an absorbing interest, which no effort of fiction can obtain, and which holds us captive as we watch him race through a few months of furious life to sudden death and an immortality of fame or infamy. So it is with the men who made our revolution, and then among the ruins of the old system built a new and better one; it is important to know and understand each and all of them. This is most true in this instance, for when we turn to Oliver Ellsworth we meet one of the most conspicuous of the makers and builders engaged in that mighty work.

Who and what was he? He was of English stock, third in descent from the ancestor who had come over to America before the first great Puritan migration had ceased on the assembling of the Long Parliament. His name is Saxon, derived from that of a Saxon village in Cambridgeshire. There is the story of his blood and race, — Saxon, English, Puritan, three words full of meaning. They bring before us the wild bands bearing down on Britain from the German forests, the slow welding of tribes and races into

the people henceforth to be known as English ; they
recall the spirit of sacrifice for conscience' sake
mingling with that older spirit of adventure, which
in the dim past had driven the long boats of the
Norseman, Dane, and Saxon across the North Sea,
and which reviving in Elizabeth's men made
prize of the American wilderness. It was a strong
race, a sturdy stock to spring from; and these
Ellsworths, complete exemplars of it, settled in
Connecticut, flourished and increased, and there, in
the town of Windsor on April 29, 1745, was
born to David Ellsworth and Jemima Leavitt, his
wife, a son whom they named Oliver. The father
was a farmer, his family neither rich nor poor,
simple in their lives, frugal in their habits, religious,
hard-working, in all their ways typifying the thousands of households who then made up what was
known as New England. Under such influences
and surroundings Oliver Ellsworth grew up. The
conditions were not easy, the outlook on life was
limited in many directions, — was sometimes hard,
sometimes narrow. But such conditions at least
bred strong men and not weaklings; they developed
virtues with the vigor of the open air about them,
and not the pallor of the cloister; they endowed
those who felt their discipline with the qualities for
strife and endurance by which nations are freed and
states founded and governed.

Among the marked characteristics of this race transplanted from the pruned and ordered garden of England to the rough wilderness of the new world was a deep reverence for learning. The ruling ambition among all families, strongest perhaps in the poorest, was that the eldest son at least should go to college and be thereafter lawyer, minister, or judge. So from the farm life and the town school at Windsor Oliver Ellsworth made his way to Yale, as was most natural, and thence after two years for some unexplained reason[1] to Princeton, where he graduated with credit.

College course finished, he returned to Windsor, studied law, was admitted to the bar, was given a small farm by his father, and upon that eked out by some trifling legal fees lived along in a thrifty, highly economical fashion, which it is said clung to him through life, and with no very brilliant prospects immediately apparent. Then one day in the Hartford Court the opportunity flies open, the native capacity suddenly becomes obvious to the vicinage, and after that the advance is steady and rapid. So rapid indeed is his rise that by the time he had passed thirty he was in the front rank and master of a practice

[1] Since this address was delivered I have learned that the " reason " was the college bell turned upside down one winter night and filled with water, which thereupon froze. The results were temporary silence on the part of the bell and the subsequent departure of young Ellsworth to the New Jersey college.

considered one of the best in Connecticut. But while
Ellsworth was thus moving forward the political
forces which were to dominate the closing years of
the century were moving too. As a boy he had
witnessed the opposition to the Stamp Act and the
rejoicing at its repeal. When he grew to manhood
it looked at first as if all was to be peaceful as of
yore, and then the low mutterings of a storm were
heard ; the apparent peace, it seemed, was only a truce,
and the clouds began to gather more darkly than before. He was still in the first flush of his young success
when news came that Boston harbor was black with
tea, and hard upon that strange defiance followed the
Boston Port Bill driving the colonies into the union
which was more perilous to England than all else.
So the American Revolution marched forward, and
Ellsworth went with it. No doubts, no hesitations,
seemingly a matter of course with him that he should
be with his country in resistance to a British policy
which meant a hopeless dependence and submission,
which would render the colonies lifeless provinces
when the aspirations of empire and the hope of a
great future were stirring unconsciously but strongly
in their hearts. The young lawyer thus drawn
into the vortex of the great movement served in the
militia, and took part in the labors of the General Assembly of which he had for some years been a member. His ability and energy thus displayed in the

work of the State carried him speedily to a larger
field. In 1777 he was chosen a delegate in Congress, and took his seat in that body the following
year.

The decline of the Continental Congress in power,
character, and influence, as compared with its remarkable strength and ability in the first session,
had already set in, but had not yet proceeded very
far. Ellsworth found among his associates his colleague Roger Sherman, Samuel Adams, Robert and
Gouverneur Morris, Witherspoon, Richard Henry Lee,
Laurens, and later John Jay, and he was entirely fit
to hold high place among men of this quality. He
was active, efficient, with large capacity sorely
needed just then for the work of administration,
and he was placed at once on committees charged
with the heaviest responsibilities. His most important service, however, was as a member of the Committee of Appeals, whose functions were judicial and
whose duty it was to hear appeals from the local
Admiralty courts. This Committee was the first imperfect beginning of the Federal judicial system from
which in process of time was to come the great organization and wide jurisdiction of the United States
Courts. It was one of the many examples of the
efforts of Congress with no proper machinery and no
adequate powers to supply the absolute necessities of
a central government; it was one of many stumbling

steps toward the making of a nation, and these abortive attempts were the hard school in which the men who met later at Philadelphia in 1787 gained the wisdom and experience which resulted in the Constitution of the United States. Thus Washington learned in the field, through many bitter years of trial and disappointment caused by the utter failure of Congress as a war-making, money-raising body, that the one thing necessary for America was a better union and a well-organized national government, — high objects to which he was to devote heart and mind and strength in the closing years of his life. By Congress, Hamilton was taught that no financial soundness or success was possible without a complete change in the methods of the confederate system and the formation of a strong central government. And in Congress likewise on this Committee of Appeals Ellsworth learned the imperative need of a Federal Judiciary and the utter helplessness of the Continental Congress to do justice or to carry out its decrees so painfully illustrated by the cause which later became famous as the Olmstead case. There in the dark confusion of revolutionary war, in that Committee of Appeals so ample in high ability, so impotent in powers of execution, were conceived the thoughts which one day would give birth to the judicial system of the United States.

Many were the services which Ellsworth performed

in Congress only to be detected by a careful examination of parliamentary journals, very cold and lifeless now, but none the less recording, in dry and formal words, deeds, efforts, and failures to which living men gave their hearts and brains and over which human passions once burned brightly enough. But Ellsworth's greatest, most patriotic service was that he remained in Congress working as best he could for the common cause until the end, — until 1782, when the great stress was over and the country was passing out of the trials of war to prepare for the equally hard trials of peace. This was no light task and no trifling sacrifice. The first Congresses had numbered in their membership all that was best and strongest in America. They set forth to the world in a series of state papers of unrivalled ability the arguments and the position of the revolting colonies, and the eyes of mankind were fixed upon them. They made the Revolution and they declared independence. Then the decline set in. The greatest man of all left Congress to command the army, and others followed him to the field. Franklin crossed the waters to seek the aid of Europe for the fighting colonies, and others followed him on the same momentous errand. Still others of the delegates left the central government for service in their States, where under the changing pressure of war they seemed to be most needed.

Thus the high ability of Congress was lowered, and then the vices of the system became more and more apparent. Congress was a legislative body striving to perform executive functions, — a plan always doomed to failure, and in this case impossible because Congress had no real power and could only make appeals to jarring and indifferent States. As Congress sank into weakness and contempt, jobbery raised its ugly head, intrigue invaded it, and smaller men took the places of the great leaders who had made the body famous. Men of the right sort shrank from it, and so decrepit did it become that toward the end it seemed little more than an additional obstacle for Washington to overcome. Very especial gratitude and honor are due, therefore, to the few men of the first rank, like Ellsworth, who clung to it to the end, extorted from it the creation of certain rude executive departments, and forced it to the point of not altogether abandoning Washington and the army. It was hard and thankless work, not shining brilliantly before the eyes of men, but all the more to be honored because done in obscurity, in the midst of distrust and contempt, and without hope either of present applause or of future reward.

As the war closed, Congress began to show signs of a revival in ability with the appearance of Hamilton and Madison and other men of a younger generation, forerunners of the constructive era which

was fast approaching. With these men Ellsworth
engaged in more welcome service than in the dark
years which had gone. But the war was over. He
had done his share and more, and in the summer of
1783 he returned to Connecticut, there to begin his
judicial career as a Judge of the Supreme Court of
Errors, which was really the upper branch of the
legislature, and afterwards as a Judge of the Supreme Court. Four years of good work passed with
much advantage to the law of the State, where the
decisions were just beginning to be reported and
preserved, and then the current of the larger life
caught him again and swept him out once more
from the quiet haven of the local bench into the
broad rough ocean of national politics.

The confederation so carefully labored over by the
revolutionary Congress had been languidly accepted
by the States and had come into a rickety existence
only to prove that it could not survive. The States
were drawing apart from each other and were torn
by internal dissensions. The outlook was black, and
the men everywhere who thought "continentally,"
saw that desperate remedies were imperative and
took counsel together. The result was the Convention which met at Philadelphia in the summer
of 1787. Connecticut was slow to move in the new
direction, but when she did so at the last moment
it was to send Roger Sherman, Oliver Ellsworth,

and William Samuel Johnson to represent her in the final effort for a better union.

We have now come to one of the three great events in Ellsworth's life, — to an act which fastens his name in history and without which the story of that eventful summer cannot be told. To trace through the records of the Convention all that he said and did in the formation of the Constitution would be impossible and for my purpose needless, because before us there is now a single achievement which rises out of the current of events as distinctly as a lofty tower on a lonely ledge, and as luminous as the light which beams forth from it over the dark waste of ocean. There were many anxious moments in that Convention, but none so anxious, none when the danger of failure and dissolution appeared so imminent, as in the contest over the basis of representation. The representatives of the larger States, the men who had thought "continentally" and had brought about the Convention, like Hamilton, Madison, Franklin, King, Wilson, and Gouverneur Morris, believed that the only solution was to frame a government for men and not for imaginary political entities called States. The jealousies and the quarrels of the old Congress with their resulting impotence and confusion had filled many of the leading minds with the belief that no government where the States as such had power could ever hope for success.

They wanted a government based on population and resting solely and directly upon the people of the entire nation. To this the small States, strong with the instinct of self-preservation, were bitterly opposed. Upon Connecticut, strange as it may seem in view of her fate as the last and surest stronghold of the extreme Federalist doctrines, the brunt of the battle in behalf of the small States fell. In this struggle Ellsworth and his eminent colleague, Roger Sherman, who more than ten years before had developed the principle of State representation, were the leaders. They both came to the Convention, therefore, imbued with the idea of resisting the over-strong centralizing tendency in which they saw at that moment great peril. At the very outset Ellsworth moved to strike from one of the preliminary resolutions the word "national" and insert as a proper title "the United States." He declared a little later, with equal terseness and force, that "the only chance of supporting a general government lies in grafting it on those of the original States;" thus laying down a principle long advocated by Sherman, which was as profound in its apprehension of the conditions as it was sound in its application to the problems of the moment. It was on this doctrine that he made his stand when the crucial question of representation confronted the Convention. Reluctantly yielding to the principle of representation according to population for the lower House, he stood out immovably for the equality of the States in the Senate. In company with Roger Sherman, who was the leader in the conflict, with Patterson of New Jersey, and Bedford of Delaware, he fought through the debate against such brilliant leaders as Hamilton and Madison, Randolph and Pinckney, Rufus King, James Wilson, and Gouverneur Morris. When the test came Georgia split her vote and the other States divided equally. The first thought was that the Convention had failed, that the hope of union had vanished. But out of that equally divided vote came a Committee of Conference, and out of that conference came the great compromise, — representation according to population in the House, equality of the States in the Senate.[1]

To show that I have not exaggerated Ellsworth's part in this momentous contest, let me cite two high authorities. Mr. Bancroft says : " There he more than any other shaped the policy which alone could have reconciled the great States and the small ones

[1] In the appendix is given a letter from my colleague the Hon. George F. Hoar which discusses fully and in the most interesting and conclusive manner the respective shares of Sherman and Ellsworth in originating and carrying through the great compromise of the Constitution which resulted in the establishment of State representation in the Senate. I desire to take this opportunity of expressing my obligations to Senator Hoar for the advice and assistance which he so constantly and so generously gave me in preparing this address, as well as for his kindness in allowing me to publish his letter.

and bound them both equally to the Union by recip-
rocal concessions. He too it was who joined with
Sherman and successfully intreated that body to bar
and bolt the doors of the United States against paper
money." [1]

Mr. Calhoun said in the Senate : " It is owing —
I speak it here in honor of New England and the
Northern States — it is owing mainly to the States
of Connecticut and New Jersey that we have a
federal instead of a national government ; that we
have the best government instead of the most
despotic and intolerable on the earth. Who were
the men of those States to whom we are indebted
for this admirable government ? I will name them.
They were Chief Justice Ellsworth, Roger Sherman,
and Judge Patterson of New Jersey. The other
States further south were blind ; they did not see
the future. But to the sagacity and coolness of
those three men, aided by a few others, but not so
prominent, we owe the present Constitution." [2]

Now exactly what was it that Ellsworth and
Sherman did ? They won their victory for equality
of State representation in one branch of Congress,
but they did far more even than this, for they and
the few who stood with them saved the Constitution itself and made it possible. Without that com-

---

[1] Century Magazine, July, 1883, p. 483.
[2] Chicago Law Times, vol. ii. p. 112.

promise there would either have been no Constitution
or the Constitution made without State representation
would have gone to pieces in the early years at the
first moment when the large States asserted their
untrammelled control of the national government.
All this is very plain to us now, but it is also very
clear that enormous importance was attached at the
moment to the construction of the upper House, for
the equality of the States in the Senate was the one
provision of the Constitution which the framers
declared could not be changed without the consent
of every State. They showed in this way their
belief that in the combination of representation of
population with representation by States the very
existence of the Constitution was involved. In
pursuance of this fundamental theory they also
provided that Senators should be elected not by
direct popular vote but by the men chosen by the
people who in the legislature constituted the State
government, and embodied the State as a political
entity. Just now there is a movement on foot to
bring about the election of Senators by direct popular vote. If successful, it will inevitably be followed
by proportional representation in the Senate, and the
most radical revolution conceivable will take place
in our form of government. We alone among the
nations possessing representative government have
fully solved the problem of an upper House resting

upon an independent basis and effective in legislation. If the Senate is placed upon the same basis
as the House and is chosen in the same way by the
same constituency, its character and meaning depart,
the States will be hopelessly weakened, the balance
of the Constitution will be destroyed, centralization
will advance with giant strides, and we shall enter
upon a period of constitutional revolution of which
the end cannot be foretold. When we contemplate
what the equality of the States in the Senate meant
at the time of the Philadelphia Convention, what it
has meant throughout our national life, and what its
overthrow would mean to-day, we realize the great
service of Sherman and Ellsworth, and how large
and enduring a place they must always hold in our
history.

Upon Ellsworth's influence in forming other parts
of the Constitution I need not dwell. It is enough
here to have shown his large share in the establishment of the vital principle of the Constitution. An
adverse fate compelled him to leave the Convention
before its adjournment and deprived him of the
satisfaction of signing his name to the great instrument. But as he came into the Convention the
champion of the rights of the States which seemed
at the moment the most serious obstacle to a better
union, he passed out of the Convention where he
had won his great victory to become the champion

of the Constitution and to give the rest of his life to
the development and enlargement of its powers and
to the upbuilding of a strong national government.
His first service to the cause was in the Convention
of Connecticut called to ratify the new Constitution.
He led the party of ratification, which fortunately
had a large majority and carried without difficulty
the adhesion of Connecticut to the new plan.
There is no better proof of the quality and effective-
ness of his speeches at that time than the fact that
Mr. Webster quoted from them in February, 1833,
when replying to Mr. Calhoun, saying, as he did
so : "I cannot do better than to leave this part of
this subject by reading the remarks upon it in the
Convention of Connecticut by Mr. Ellsworth, a
gentleman, Sir, who has left behind him on the
records of the government of his country proofs of
the clearest intelligence and of the deepest sagacity,
as well as of the utmost purity and integrity of
character."

When the necessary number of States had ratified
the Constitution and the new government was ready
to start, Connecticut sent, as one of her first representatives in the Senate, the man to whom that body
largely owed its existence. Ellsworth was one of
the eight Senators who appeared in New York on
the 4th of March, 1789. There he waited patiently
for six weeks until the quorum of Congress had

gathered, there he took part in the inauguration of Washington, and there he began a service as Senator which was to last for seven years.

Once more time and space forbid me to trace in detail the career which makes Ellsworth one of the great names in the history of the Senate. In all that came before the Senate in those formative years, he took a leading part, and it is not easy to conceive, in this day so rich in traditions and precedents, the absolute vacancy which confronted the first Senators when they assembled in New York in the spring of 1789. There were no laws, no rules, no forms, no customs, no practice, no government, nothing but the clauses of a freshly drawn, uninterpreted, untried Constitution. All was to do. Even the enacting clauses of bills had to be formulated by somebody, the somebody chanced to be Ellsworth, and the manner in which the President and other officers of the government were to be addressed was only settled after long debate. In those momentous years the great measures and the far-reaching policies which founded the nation and organized the country stand out on the pages of history for all men to see and admire. But the countless little measures and decisions of the passing day by which the firm mass of habits, customs, and traditions, often more powerful in holding the respect of men, and guarding a country from revolution than many great measures of state, were then founded deep and strong. In both fields Ellsworth was a leader. His was one of the guiding minds in devising the delicate machinery, the small wheels and nicely adjusted mechanism upon which, although hidden from sight, all government moves. And he also stands out conspicuous as one of the chief constructive legislators of a great period of construction, for it was he who drafted the Judiciary Act, upon which the judicial system of the United States has rested ever since, and to which all subsequent legislation for the judiciary has been but extension and amendment. This was his second service to his country, so large in its scope as to give him a lasting place in our legislative history, even as the equality of the States in the Senate is his enduring monument in the history of our Constitution. Outside the Senate chamber too, as well as within, he fully performed those duties which he conceived the Constitution imposed upon the Senators as the only constitutional advisers of the Executive. He was no stranger to the President. His services in the Continental Congress and in the Convention had made him known to Washington, to whom Ellsworth's high qualities of mind and character strongly appealed. When the President made his tour of New England at the beginning of his administration, he stopped at Ellsworth's house, and we get a very human, very illuminating glimpse of him there playing with the children of the Senator and singing a song to them.   Through all the period of Ellsworth's service in the Senate he was one of the chosen group of men upon whom Washington leaned, whose advice he sought, and whose suggestions were always welcome.   A simple incident connected with one of the gravest questions of the time, and related by one of Ellsworth's grandsons, will show at once his grasp of our foreign policy, and the part he played in the administration of Washington :

"In January, 1794, a majority of the House of Representatives was prepared to declare war with Great Britain notwithstanding the defenceless state of the country.   Mr. Ellsworth, though not in the Cabinet, was in the confidence of Washington, and kept a watchful eye on every subject and circumstance connected with the affairs of the administration and the welfare of the country.   He was confident that war could be avoided.   To accomplish this purpose he, with Governor Strong, Mr. King, and Mr. Cabot, his intimate and confidential associates, then in the Senate, in February or March, 1794, met to consult, and, if possible, devise some course to secure the country from the awful disaster which seemed inevitable, all argument in Congress having become ineffectual with the majority.   They determined upon the expedient of a mission to England forthwith to open a negotiation for a treaty on the point in controversy between the two nations. They agreed to recommend the nomination of John Jay, Alexander Hamilton, and perhaps one other, whose name is unknown to the writer, for that mission. Mr. Ellsworth was designated to confer with the President on the subject. He related to him the confidential consultation held in relation to the alarming condition of the country. . . .

"General Washington listened to the communication with apparent deep concern, and after a long and familiar conversation on the subject said :

" ' Well, what can be done, Mr. Ellsworth ? '

" Mr. Ellsworth informed him of the result of their consultation, ' that a Minister Plenipotentiary be sent to England forthwith,' and named the persons selected by himself and friends for the mission.

" It was apparent that to the President this was a new project.

" At the close of the interview the President said : ' Well, sir, I will take this subject into consideration.'

" Mr. Jay was nominated on the 16th of April, and although this measure was scarcely suspected by Congress, and a majority of the House of Representatives was opposed to it, the nomination was approved by the Senate by a vote of 18 to 8. The

result of the mission, notwithstanding the intrigues
of the French Ministry, was the well-known Jay
treaty.

" After the treaty was approved by the Senate the
hostility toward it seemed more alarming than ever,
and while the President had the subject under consideration the anxiety of Mr. Ellsworth increased
with the delay. He thought the least appearance of
indecision in him would be ruin to the country, that
every day's procrastination increased the dangers of
the republic. . . . During this state of suspense by
reason of General Washington's delay to sign the
treaty, Mr. Ellsworth walked the hall in the most
intense anxiety as to the result, and scarcely closed
his eyes in sound sleep for several nights.

" While the treaty was under discussion, Mr. Livingston offered a resolution ' That the President be
requested to lay before the House a copy of the
instructions given to the Minister of the United
States who negotiated the treaty, together with the
documents, etc., with the exception of such papers as
any existing negotiations may render improper.'
This was adopted (62 to 37), and was sent to the
President. The members of the Cabinet unanimously
advised the President not to comply with the resolution. Mr. Ellsworth was requested to draw up an
argument showing that the papers could not be constitutionally demanded by the House of Representa-

tives, and a message was sent by the President in accordance therewith." [1]

Forbidden, as I have said, by the limitations of an address to show what Mr. Ellsworth was as a Senator by tracing his work in detail from year to year, I cannot leave this most important part of his career without trying to indicate by other means what his position in the Senate was, and what he meant to the men he met there. He was constant in attendance, shared in all debates, took part in all business and in the making of all laws. Influence in the Senate always rests largely upon these somewhat humdrum qualities of attention, industry, and activity, and how potent Ellsworth's influence was is sharply shown by a little anecdote. Aaron Burr, who served nearly six years with Ellsworth, said of him, " If he should chance to spell the name of the Deity with two D's, it would take the Senate three weeks to expunge the superfluous letter."

But we have a witness on this point far more important and far more elaborate than Burr. William Maclay was a Senator from Pennsylvania during the first two years of our government. At a period when the Senate sat behind closed doors and had no records of debates, he kept a careful diary narrating their proceedings. Historically therefore this diary is valuable, and constitutes the

---

[1] The New York Evening Post, July 3, 1876.

chief claim of its writer to the notice of posterity.
Senator Maclay's editor and descendant asserts that
his ancestor was the true founder of the Democratic
party, an honor usually accorded to Jefferson. If
consistent opposition to every measure proposed,
if suspicion and hostility directed unsparingly at
Washington, Adams, Hamilton, and every one who
supported or acted with them, if general dissatisfac-
tion with everything that was done entitle a man
to be considered the founder of the Democratic
party, Mr. Maclay certainly preceded Mr. Jefferson
in all these directions and his descendant's claim of
glory for him is fully made out. He naturally took
a very dark view of Ellsworth, and therefore his unwilling testimony to that gentleman's place and
power in the Senate is most valuable. From the
diary we learn that Ellsworth dealt with every
point of procedure, with the powers of the Vice-
President, the manner of receiving the House and
the style of the enacting clause. To Ellsworth we
learn was due the resolution by which the Senate
system of considering bills in Committee of the
Whole without the Vice-President's leaving the
chair was established. Ellsworth defended a large
bench of judges, and Maclay says of the Judiciary
Act, Ellsworth's great work in our early legislation,
" This vile bill was a child of his." Maclay also
thought that this bill would " blow up the Consti-

tution," but posterity knows that it became one of the bulwarks of our great charter. Again it was the Connecticut Senator who in an elaborate speech of high ability asserted that the President's power of removal was absolute and the power of appointment alone limited, — a doctrine finally accepted by the Senate after eighty years of intermittent discussion, legislation, and debate. On the same authority we find that Ellsworth did not confine himself to legal and constitutional questions, but presented the bill to organize the territories, and had a leading part in measures relating to the army and tariff. It is a remarkable record. Consider carefully this dry list of momentous questions, and then you realize how the influence and power of this statesman, long since dead, are felt, more than a century after his work was done, in the daily conduct of the business of our great government.

And what are the comments of the diarist who records so many deeds and credits such large activities to a single man ? They are interesting and in the broadest sense instructive. He says that Ellsworth leads, that he is all powerful and eloquent in debate, and that he is, although "endless," really a man of great ingenuity and ability. On one occasion Maclay said to him, " The man must knit his net close that can catch you ; but you trip sometimes." Yet at the same time he says of Ellsworth

that " it is truly surprising to me, the pains he will
display to varnish over villany and to give roguery
effect without avowed license." He describes Ellsworth as a tool of " Hamilton and his crew," whom
he regarded as totally corrupt, and toward the close
of the session says, " the man has abilities, but
abilities without candor and integrity are characteristics of the devil." What a picture is here!
At the very dawn of the Republic a President
weak, ambitious, inclined to monarchy, the tool of
designing men, — such according to the diarist was
George Washington. The Vice-President also leaning to monarchy, violent, arbitrary, absurd, — such, if
we believe Maclay, was John Adams. Then there
are " Hamilton and his crew," corrupt, dangerous,
battening on the public treasury, with an equally
corrupt set supporting the Secretary in Congress.
The Senate is quite as bad ; it is deeply corrupted,
false to freedom and to democratic ideals. One of
its great leaders is a man engaged in " varnishing
over roguery " and " destitute of candor and integrity." *Ex pede Herculem!* If Ellsworth was a
man of this kind, what must the other Senators
have been ?

How false it all is ! How well we know now the
greatness, the unspotted purity of Washington, the
fiery courage and unbending patriotism of Adams,
the vast constructive genius of Hamilton, the com-

manding abilities, the lasting services, the unsullied
honor of Ellsworth! What a lesson too is here if we
will but take the trouble to learn it! I never remember the time when I have not heard the Senate
of the moment described as at its lowest point, as
having fallen far down from the high level of the
earlier and better days. Then I read Maclay and
take heart, for if he is right and our Senate and our
government were such as he described, and if the
bitter critics of the moment are also right and we
are worse now than in the earlier and better days,
then indeed has the impossible come to pass, for the
Republic still survives, greater and more powerful,
more honored at home and abroad than ever before.
Then I feel sure that the critics of this kind, past and
present, must be wrong, for if they were not the Republic would have died. The Maclays, like the poor,
are always with us, sole proprietors of righteousness,
undisturbed by any outcry against their self-imposed
monopoly. They have their value, no doubt, although
their own estimate of their worth is probably beyond the market price. I would not willingly speak
harshly of any living successor of Maclay, but of the
dead critic fronting the merciless gaze of history,
something may be said. Malignity easily assumes
the garb of a noble independence, while envy, hatred,
and all uncharitableness delight to masquerade in the
guise of the most loved and admired virtues. As we

see now from the cool eminence of a new century the
distant figure of Oliver Ellsworth rise up clear and
serene, his brow laurelled with good deeds done for
his country, his memory fragrant with patriotism,
honor, and noble thoughts, it is well to turn to
Maclay's diary and to remember that this dead statesman fought once in the dust of the arena, was thus
attacked and slandered and misjudged even by one
who stood near him. The career of the statesman
and jurist shines all the brighter by the contrast, and
History with her calm voice, as she unrolls the page
and spreads the whole record before our eyes, bids us
even now to be temperate in judgment, to be tolerant
as well as just, to look out upon the present with a
kindly as well as a searching gaze and above all to
take heart and hold fast to a deep and abiding faith
in the American people and in the Republic of our
love.

I have dwelt at length on Ellsworth's services in
the Senate, and yet am conscious that I have not done
justice to it or shown in such measure as ought to be
shown his attitude upon many great questions, especially of foreign relations, where he gave all his influence and support to the neutrality policy, to resistance
to the encroachments of France, and to the maintenance of peace with England, culminating in the Jay
treaty, for which he did battle in the angry conflict
that arose over its provisions. But I must be con-

tent with the effort I have made to bring out in relief the brilliancy of his Senatorial service, and the great part he played in the formative period of our national government.

The struggle over the treaty with England marked indeed the close of his work in the Senate. The rejection of Rutledge by the Senate and the refusal of Cushing to accept the Chief Justiceship made it more than ever important to fill that great post with a man who would command not only the support of the Federalists, but the confidence of the country as well. After much deliberation Washington turned to Ellsworth, and appointed him to the vacant place. He accepted with reluctance the duty which had come to him unsought, and was sworn in as Chief Justice on the 8th of March, 1796. He came to his great office well qualified both by professional training and by experience as a statesman and law-maker. He served well and efficiently, and maintained and strengthened the character of the court. Yet it was not as Chief Justice that his best work was done. Ellsworth did good service in admiralty cases, with which he was particularly familiar, and in defining and settling the jurisdiction of the Court. His most famous opinion was in favor of the doctrine of perpetual allegiance, which has since been abandoned. But there was no case where he rendered a decision which is at all comparable in im-

portance with his achievements in the Constitutional
Convention or in the Senate of the United States.
In his years of service as Chief Justice the great constitutional questions by the decision of which the
national principle was to be built up and extended
did not meet him. They were to be reserved for
the touch of a mightier hand than his. Yet on the
bench of the Supreme Court, although he did not
originate doctrines nor leave an enduring mark upon
our history as he had done when delegate and Senator, he nevertheless met thoroughly and well all the
requirements of his high place.

Had he remained Chief Justice, there can be no
doubt that he would have left a very great reputation, but a call came to him after four years of
judicial service which he could not refuse. We
became engaged in actual hostilities, though not in
declared war, with France. The Federal leaders
were for war, but John Adams determined to make
one more effort for peace. He profoundly believed,
as Washington had believed, that the young nation
must be kept from war if possible. In this he was
greatly right, but he was right in such a wrong way
that, while he saved the country from grave danger,
he shattered his party in doing it. His first step
was a blunder, for he named William Vans Murray
alone to re-open relations with France. Something
stronger than that was needed if the confirmation of

the Senate was to be obtained, and the President, quickly conscious of his error and of impending defeat, added Ellsworth and Patrick Henry, for whom Governor Davie of North Carolina was afterwards substituted, to the Commission. Thus fortified, the Commission was confirmed. Ellsworth's health and inclination alike opposed an acceptance which involved not only a long journey and trying responsibilities, but also a sharp difference of opinion with the other Federalist chiefs, the friends with whom he had labored for years. But he felt now, as he had felt at the time of the Jay treaty, that peace was essential to the young Republic and its unformed government, and that no honorable effort should be spared to preserve it. The request of the President came to him as an order to a high duty, and such an order it was not in him to disobey.

On November 3, 1799, the envoys sailed from Newport, and on the 27th they reached Lisbon. For those days the voyage was quick, but brief as the interval had been it had sufficed to change the face of the European world. The 18th Brumaire had come and gone, the Directory had fallen, and Napoleon was master of France. Warned by the experience of their predecessors, Ellsworth and Davie proceeded slowly toward France, and sent a letter to announce their coming. Talleyrand was still in office, as ready no doubt to be bribed as before, but his new master was not an idiot like the Directory, which for a little illicit gain had been ready apparently to bring on war with America. The utter folly of making war on the United States at that moment was indeed obvious at once to Napoleon. The message went back to the American envoys that "they were awaited with impatience and would be received with warmth." Ellsworth and Davie pressed forward, reached Paris on March 2, 1800, met Murray there, and in a few days were engaged in negotiations with a Commission appointed by the First Consul and headed by Joseph Bonaparte.

There is a tradition that when Napoleon's piercing gaze fell upon Ellsworth at the audience given to the American Commissioners soon after their arrival, he said, "I must make a treaty with that man." The story may readily be believed, for different as Ellsworth was in his sober attire from those about him, upon whom the light of the coming glories of the empire was already beginning to shine, he was a man certain to attract attention anywhere. He was tall and erect. He had a strong face, and large penetrating blue eyes looked out fearlessly upon the world from beneath heavy arched brows. His expression was pleasant and his presence commanding, instinct with the dignity of one who had presided over a great court. He was particular and very quiet in his dress, with his hair powdered in a fashion even then becoming antique, and he still wore silk stockings and silver knee-buckles after the mode of a vanishing period. Generally absorbed in meditation, often talking to himself when he walked or rode, his thoughts were nevertheless so ordered and disciplined, that when he spoke his words came rapidly and earnestly as he marshalled his arguments and stated his opinions. Altogether a stately figure, we may say, one very typical of a strong race with an obvious force of character and intelligence which was perceived at once by the greatest genius of the time, as his glance fell upon the sober dress and calm face of the New England statesman and jurist, descendant of many Puritans.

The negotiations thus begun, proceeded smoothly enough. The revival of the old treaties of alliance demanded by the French and the indemnities insisted upon by the Americans for the captures made by the privateers of the Republic which had brought about actual hostilities were found incapable of adjustment. The extreme Federalists at home thought the negotiations should have ended then, but Ellsworth laid aside the irreconcilable points for a more convenient season, and with his colleagues made a treaty by which France agreed to pay her debts to the United States, and the commercial relations of the two countries were arranged. Free ships were to make free goods; the neutral flag was to protect the cargo, and commerce was made reciprocally free on the footing of the most favored nation. The work was chiefly done by Ellsworth, and can be summed up in a word. He abandoned the discussion of the old grievances, and made a new treaty covering similar questions in the future, which was calculated to stimulate the expansion of our trade and which averted war. The treaty was not thought a very brilliant one at the time, but it is easy to see now that it was eminently wise. It was infinitely more important to the United States to be rid of the treaty of 1778, than to secure indemnities for the captures of the French privateers. By Ellsworth's policy we shook ourselves free from an entangling alliance, and the indemnities, a mere matter of money, found a later settlement. These questions thus postponed were the crucial points of the negotiation. The treaty itself was well enough for commercial purposes, but its great work was in stopping hostilities and assuring an honorable peace, which was of great moment to our new government. It also brought about a friendly understanding and opened the way to the Louisiana treaty, an inestimable benefit. Altogether it was good work well done, the work of a statesman far-seeing, strong, and courageous, who looked beneath the surface and was guided by general principles and by a settled policy.

The treaty was signed on the 30th of September,

1800, and was followed by a fête given to the American envoys, which was more significant of the desire of France to be on good terms with the American Republic than anything that had happened. I will borrow Mr. Bancroft's account of this now forgotten event, which made much noise in its day, and was carefully noted by European observers of contemporary politics and of the signs of the times.

" The French government resolved to give them on their departure the clearest proof of the enduring good will of France for the American Republic. It chanced that Joseph Bonaparte, who was the richest of the family, possessed a magnificent country-seat at Morfontaine, which lies some leagues from Paris on the road to Havre. There, on their way, at the château of Joseph Bonaparte, under whose lead the treaty with the United States had been concluded on the part of France, the American ministers were invited to be the guests at a farewell festival before their embarkation.

" The American envoys arrived at the village of Morfontaine about two o'clock in the afternoon, and found there a large number of the French magistrates already assembled. At four o'clock Napoleon Bonaparte, the First Consul of France, . . . entered the château amidst salutes from artillery and bands of music. During the evening the castle and adjacent

buildings were brilliantly illuminated. The approval
of the treaty by the First Consul, of which assurance
was formally given about eight o'clock in the evening,
was followed by the firing of cannon. After this the
guests, about one hundred and fifty in number, were
seated at tables in three large halls. To the largest
of them the name was given of the 'Hall of the
Union.' It was superbly decorated with wreaths
and numerous inscriptions commemorating the 4th
of July, 1776, and other days famous for important
actions in America during their struggle for independence. The initial letters of France and America
were inscribed in many places. The City of Philadelphia, which was then the seat of the Federal
Congress, and Havre, which was the port for
the embarkation of the American ministers, were
represented with an angel on the wing from
Havre to Philadelphia, bearing an olive branch.
The second hall was called the 'Hall of Washington,' and was adorned with his bust and the French
and American flags standing side by side. The
third hall was called the 'Hall of Franklin,' whose
bust was its ornament. All the decorations were
especially designed to commemorate the independence of the United States and French liberty.
In that spirit the First Consul, Napoleon, then just
thirty-one years of age, gave as the first toast: 'The
memory of those who have fallen in the defence of

French and American liberty.' The second toast was proposed by the Third Consul, Lebrun: 'The union of America with the powers of the North to enforce respect for the liberties of the seas.' Last of all, Cambacères, the Second Consul, in honor of the President of the United States, proposed 'The successor of Washington.' After supper there was a brilliant and ingenious display of fireworks in the garden. Next followed an exquisite concert of music, and about midnight the private theatre was opened for the performance of two short comedies, in which the best of the actors and actresses from Paris played the parts. At the conclusion of one of the plays a song complimentary to the United States was sung; and thus the evening came to an end."

The Chief Justice was not well when he left the United States, and the Atlantic voyage followed by a winter journey through Spain and by the cares and anxiety of the negotiation broke his health down completely. Before leaving France he resigned the Chief Justiceship, and it was with but slight hopes of improvement that he crossed to England. There, however, contrary to expectation he grew rapidly better. The repose after so many labors, the climate, the attentions which he received from bench and bar, and a congenial society, all helped him to recovery. His stay in England, free from care, diversified by little journeys, one among others to the cradle of his race, made one of the pleasantest periods in a laborious life. He stayed in London and its neighborhood until the spring of 1801, and then returned to America and to his home in Windsor. But complete withdrawal from public affairs was not to be his portion. He had scarcely settled down in his well-loved home when he was appointed again to his old place in the Governor's Council, which still constituted the Supreme Court of Errors of the State. It was a duty to be performed, and weary and worn as he was, he accepted it. There he served, after his life-long habit, faithfully and well, despite severe and recurring attacks of disease. The old judicial system was changed in 1807, and the Chief Justiceship under the new arrangement was offered to Ellsworth. He at first consented, but then withdrew his acceptance. It was too late for more work, for the performance of further duties. The hand of death was on him, and on the 27th of November, 1807, he died at Windsor.

So a life filled with high service came to an end. Even imperfectly as I have traced it we can see, I think, what manner of man he was. As I have studied Oliver Ellsworth and come to know him, it seems to me as if he must have been the type of man Milton had in mind when he described a free commonwealth. "What government," he asks,

" comes nearer to the precept of Christ than a free commonwealth, wherein they who are the greatest are perpetual servants and drudges to the public at their own cost and charges; neglect their own affairs, yet are not elevated above their brethren; live soberly in their families, walk the street as other men, may be spoken to freely, familiarly, friendly, without adoration?"

After such fashion he passed through his great public career. Distinguished at the bar, he brought the training of a lawyer to his work as a statesman. Most eminent as a maker of constitutions and laws, he carried his large experience with him to adorn the bench, where he occupied the highest place. As a diplomatist he united all his powers as statesman and jurist in making a treaty which, dust to-day, was one of the momentous events in the early years of conflict and peril. In the history of Connecticut he stands side by side with his illustrious colleague Roger Sherman, whom he modestly says he took for his model, and who was one of the most original, most resolute, and most far-seeing men of that great period.

In the history of the United States the vital compromise which secured the existence of the Constitution is branded with his name, and the great system of the Federal courts and of the jurisprudence of the United States bears upon its foundation

stone the name of the lawyer who drafted the first
Judiciary Act. "Ellsworth was one of the pillars
of Washington's administration," said John Adams.
Can there be a better summary of his life or higher
praise of a public man than that simple sentence?
The man whom Washington trusted we may safely
revere, and he needs no monument to recall his
memory, for that is safe while the Constitution of
his country and the administration of her laws live
on in strength and power, the bulwarks of the great
Republic.

DANIEL WEBSTER

HIS ORATORY AND HIS INFLUENCE[1]

STATUES and monuments can justify their existence on only two grounds, — the nature of the subject they commemorate or as works of art. They ought, of course, to possess both qualifications in the fullest measure. Theoretically, at least, a great art should ever illustrate and should always have a great subject. But art cannot command at will a fit subject, and it is therefore fortunately true that if the art be great it is its own all-sufficient warrant for existence. That Michael Angelo's unsurpassed figure called "Meditation" should be in theory a portrait statue and bear the name of one of the most worthless of the evil Medicean race is, after all, of slight moment. The immortal art remains to delight and to uplift every one who looks upon it with considerate eyes ; and it matters little that all the marvellous figures which the chapel of the Medici enshrines were commanded and carved in order to

[1] An address delivered in Washington, January 18, 1900, before the President of the United States and his Cabinet, the Supreme Court and the Congress of the United States on the occasion of the unveiling of a statue of Daniel Webster.

keep alive the memory of a remarkable family steeped in crime and a curse to every people among whom they came. On the other hand, hard as it often is, we can endure bad art if there be no question that the great man or the shining deed deserves the commemoration of bronze or marble. But when the art is bad and the subject unworthy or ephemeral, then the monument, as was said of Sir John Vanbrugh's palaces, is simply a heavy load to the patient earth and an offence to the eyes of succeeding generations.

In these days the world sins often and grievously in this way, and is much given to the raising of monuments, too frequently upon trifling provocation. Yet the fault lies not in the mere multiplication of monuments. The genius of Greece and of the Renaissance multiplied statues, and very wisely, too, because art then was at once splendid and exuberant. But great sculptors and painters are as few now as they were plentiful in the age of Phidias or of Michael Angelo and Donatello, and we erect statues and monuments with a prodigal hand chiefly because we are very rich, and because mechanical appliances have made easy the moulding of metal and the carving of stone. It behooves us, therefore, not only to choose with care artists who can give us worthy work for posterity to look upon, but also to avoid recklessness in rearing monuments upon slight

grounds. At present there seems no disposition to
heed these salutary principles. The cities and towns
of Europe and of England swarm with modern
statues and monuments as a rule ugly or commonplace, too often glaring and vulgar, and very frequently erected to the memory and the glory of the
illustrious obscure and of the parish hero. We
Americans sin less often, I think, in these respects
than the Old World, but we follow their practice
none the less and with many melancholy results.
We should break away from the present example of
Europe and realize that the erection of an enduring
monument in a public place is a very serious matter.
We should seek out the best artists and should permit
no monuments to deeds or to men who do not deserve
them and who will not themselves be monumental
in history and before the eyes of posterity. Here in
Washington, especially, we should bear this principle
in mind, for this is the city of the nation, and it
should have no place for local glories or provincial
heroes. Yet even here we have been so careless that
while we have given space to one or more statues of
estimable persons, the fact of whose existence will
be known only by their effigies, we have found as yet
no place for a statue of Hamilton, the greatest constructive statesman of our history, or of the great
soldier whose genius made the campaign of Vicksburg
rival that of Ulm.

To-day no such doubts or criticisms need haunt or perplex us. We can thank the artist who has conceived, and most unreservedly can we thank the generous and public-spirited citizen of New Hampshire who has given, the statue which we unveil this morning. If any one among our statesmen has a title to a statue in Washington, it is Daniel Webster, for this is the national capital, and no man was ever more national in his conceptions and his achievements than he. Born and bred in New Hampshire, which first elected him to the House, he long represented Massachusetts, the State of his adoption, in the Congress of the United States, and thus two historic Commonwealths cherish his memory. But much as he loved them both, his public service was given to the nation, and so given that no man doubts his title to a statue here in this city. Why is there neither doubt nor question as to Webster's right to this great and lasting honor half a century after his death? If we cannot answer this question so plainly that he who runs may read, then we unveil our own ignorance when we unveil his statue and leave the act without excuse. I shall try, briefly, to put the answer to this essential question into words. We all feel in our hearts and minds the reply that should be made. It has fallen to me to give expression to that feeling.

What, then, are the real reasons for the great

place which Webster fills in our history? I do not propose to answer this question by reviewing the history of his time or by retelling his biography. Both history and biography contain the answer, yet neither is the answer. They are indeed much more, for they carry with them, of necessity, everything concerning the man, his strength and his weakness, his virtues and his defects, all the criticism, all the differences of opinion which such a career was sure to arouse and which such an influence upon his country and upon its thought, upon his own time and upon the future, was equally sure to generate. There is a place for all this, but not here to-day. We do not raise a monument to WEBSTER upon debatable grounds, and thus make it the silent champion of one side of a dead controversy. We do not set up his statue because he changed his early opinions upon the tariff, because he remained in Tyler's Cabinet after that President's quarrel with the Whigs, or because he made upon the 7th of March a speech about which men have differed always and probably always will differ. Still less do we place here his graven image in memory of his failings or his shortcomings. History, with her cool hands, will put all these things into her scales and mete out her measure with calm, unflinching eyes. But this is History's task, not ours, and we raise this statue on other grounds.

"Not ours to gauge the more or less,
    The will's defect, the blood's excess,
    The earthy humors that oppress
        The radiant mind.
    His greatness, not his littleness,
    Concerns mankind."

To his greatness, then, we rear this monument. In what does that greatness, acknowledged by all, unquestioned and undenied by any one, consist ? Is it in the fact that he held high office ? He was a brilliant Member of Congress ; for nineteen years a great Senator ; twice Secretary of State. But " the peerage solicited him, not he the peerage." Tenure of office is nothing, no matter how high the place. A name recorded in the list of holders of high office is little better than one writ in water if the office holding be all. We do not raise this statue to the Member of Congress, to the Senator of the United States, or to the Secretary of State, but to Daniel Webster. That which concerns us is what he did with these great places which were given to him ; for to him, as to all others, they were mere opportunities. What did he do with these large opportunities ? Still more, what did he do with the splendid faculties which nature gave him ? In the answer lies the greatness which lifts him out of the ranks and warrants statues to his memory.

First, then, of those qualities which he inherited from the strong New England stock that gave him

birth, and which Nature, the fairy who stands by
every cradle, poured out upon him. How generous,
how lavish she was to that "infant crying in the
night, that infant crying for the light" in the rough
frontier village of New Hampshire a hundred and
eighteen years ago! She gave him the strong, un-
tainted blood of a vigorous race — the English
Puritans — who in the New World had been for five
generations fighting the hard battle of existence
against the wilderness and the savage. His father
was a high type of this class, a farmer and a frontiersman, a pioneer and Indian fighter, then a soldier
of the Revolution. On guard the night of Arnold's
treason, Washington in that dark hour declared that
Captain Webster was a man who could be trusted;
simple words, but an order of merit higher and more
precious than any glowing ribbon or shining star.
So fathered and so descended, the child was endowed
with physical attributes at once rare and inestimable.
When developed into manhood he was of commanding stature and seemed always even larger and taller
than he really was. Strong, massive, and handsome, he stood before his fellow-men looking upon
them with wonderful eyes, if we may judge from all
that those who saw him tell us. "Dull anthracite
furnaces under overhanging brows, waiting only to
be blown," says Carlyle; and those deep-set, glowing
eyes pursue us still in all that we read of Webster,

8

just as they seemed to haunt every one who looked upon them in life. When in a burst of passion or of solemn eloquence he fixed his eyes upon his hearers, each man in a vast audience felt that the burning glance rested upon him alone and that there was no escape. Above the eyes were the high, broad brow and the great leonine head ; below them the massive jaw and the firm mouth " accurately closed." All was in keeping. No one could see him and not be impressed. The English navvy with his " There goes a king," Sydney Smith, who compared Webster to " a walking cathedral," and the great Scotchman, harsh in judgment and grudging of praise, who set him down as a " Parliamentary Hercules," all alike felt the subduing force of that personal presence. Look upon some of the daguerreotypes taken of him in his old age, when the end was near. I think the face is one of the most extraordinary, in its dark power and tragic sadness, of all the heads which any form of human portraiture has preserved. So imposing was he that when he rose to speak, even on the most unimportant occasions, he looked, as Parton says, like " Jupiter in a yellow waistcoat," and even if he uttered nothing but commonplaces, or if he merely sat still, such was his " might and majesty," that all who listened felt that every phrase was charged with deep and solemn meaning, and all who gazed at him were awed and impressed.

Add to all this a voice of great compass, with deep organ tones, and we have an assemblage of physical gifts concentrated in this one man which would have sufficed to make even common abilities seem splendid.

But the abilities were far from common. The intellect within answered to the outward vesture. Very early does it appear, when we hear of "Webster's boy" lifted upon a stone wall to read or recite to the teamsters stopping to water their horses near the Webster farm. They were a rough, hardy set, but there was something in the child with the large dark eyes that held them and made them listen. And the father, gallant and quite pathetic soul, with a dumb and very manifest love of higher things, resolved that this boy should have all the advantages which had been denied to himself. Like the Scottish peasants, who toiled and moiled and pinched and saved that their boy might go to the university to cultivate learning on a little oatmeal, so with many silent sacrifices Ebenezer Webster sent his son to school and college and gave him every opportunity the little State afforded. The boy was not slow to make the most of all that was thus opened to him. The dormant talents grew and burgeoned in the congenial soil. Love of books made him their reader and master. Rare powers of memory and of acquisition showed themselves; a strong imagination led him to the great makers of verse, and natural taste took him to the masters of style, both in English and Latin. When he passed out of college his capacity for work brought him hardly earned pittances as a school-teacher, and then carried him through the toilsome, early stages of the law. As he advanced, the eager delight of acquisition was succeeded, as is ever the case, by the passionate desire for expression, and soon the signs come of the power of analysis, of the instinct of lucid statement at once so clear and so forcible as to amount to demonstration. We see before us as we study those early years the promise of the great master of words to whom a whole nation was one day to listen.

And with all these gifts, physical and mental, possibly, but not necessarily, the outcome of them all, we see that Webster had that indefinable quality which for lack of a better name we call "charm." He exercised a fascination upon men and women alike, upon old and young, upon all who came in contact with him. When as a boy he returned from the country fair, his mother said to him, "Daniel, what did you do with your quarter?" "Spent it." "Ezekiel, what did you do with yours?" "Lent it to Daniel." As with the elder brother then, so it was through life. Webster strode along the pathway of his great career in solemn state, and there were always people about him ready to lend to him and to give to him; not money, merely, but love and

loyalty and service, ungrudging and unreasoning,
without either question or hope of reward. A wonderful power this, as impalpable as the tints of the
rainbow, and yet as certain as the sun which paints
the colors on the clouds and makes all mankind look
toward them for the bow of hope and promise.

So he went on and up from the college, the school-
house, and the country jury, until he stood at the
head of the American bar before the Supreme Court
of the nation.   On and up he went, from the early
florid orations of youth until he became the first
orator of his time, without superior or rival.   He
frightened and disappointed his father by refusing
the safe harbor of a clerk of court, and strode onward and upward until he stood at the head of the
Senate and directed from the State Department the
foreign policy of his country. Up and on from
the farmhouse and the schoolhouse, from the stone
wall whence he read to the rude audience of teamsters, to the days when thousands hung upon his
words, when he created public opinion and shaped
the political thought of his nation.   What a triumphant progress it was, and of it all what now remains
to make men say fifty years after his death that he
merits not only a statue but lasting remembrance?
Is it to be found in his success as a great advocate
and lawyer, the acknowledged head of his profession?
There is nothing which demands or calls forth greater

intellectual powers or larger mental resources than the highest success at the bar, and yet no reputation is more evanescent. The decisions of judges remain and become part of the law of the land, lasting monuments of the learning and the thought which brought them forth. But the arguments which enlightened courts, which swayed juries, upon which public attention was fixed in admiration, fade almost in the hour, while the brilliant lawyer who uttered them soon becomes a tradition and a memory.

We must look beyond his triumphs at the bar to find the Webster of history. Beyond his work as a lawmaker, also, for, although he had a lion's share in the legislation of his time, it is not as a constructive statesman that he lives for us to-day. In the first rank as a lawmaker and as a lawyer, something very great must remain behind if we can readily and justly set aside such claims as these and say the highest remembrance rests on other grounds. Yet such is the case; and the first, but the lesser, of these other grounds is his power of speech. Eminent as a legislator, still more distinguished as a lawyer, Webster was supreme as an orator. I had occasion some years ago to make a very careful study of Webster's speeches and orations. I read with them, and in strict comparison, all that was best in Greek, Latin, French, and English oratory, and all that is best and finest — I do not say all that is fine and good — is to be found in those four languages. Webster stood the comparison without need of deduction or apology. I do not think that I am influenced by national feeling, for my object was to exclude the historical as well as the personal valuation, and to reach a real estimate. When all was done, it seemed to me that Webster was unequalled. I am sure that he is unsurpassed as an orator. There was no need for him to put pebbles in his mouth to cure stammering, or to rehearse his speeches on the seashore in conflict with the noise of the waves. He had from the hand of nature all the graces of person and presence, of voice and delivery, which the most exacting critic could demand, and these natural gifts were trained, enhanced, and perfected by years of practice in the Senate, the court room, and before the people. In what he said he always had distinction — rarest of qualities — and he had also the great manner, just as Milton has it in verse. To lucid statement, to that simplicity in discussion which modern times demand for practical questions, to nervous force, he added, at his best, wealth of imagery, richness of diction, humor, and pathos, all combined with the power of soaring on easy wing to the loftiest flights of eloquence. Above all, he had that highest quality, the " σπουδαιότην " or high and excellent seriousness which Aristotle sets down as one of the supreme virtues of poetry and without which neither oratory nor poetry can attain supremacy.

Charles Fox was the author of the famous aphorism that " no good speech ever read well." This is the declaration in epigrammatic form that the speech which is prepared like an essay and read or recited, which, in other words, is literature before it is oratory, is not thoroughly good; and of the soundness of the doctrine there can be, I think, no doubt. But this proposition is not without its dangers. Charles Fox lived up to his own principle. He was, in my opinion, the greatest of English orators at the moment of speech, but he is little read and seldom quoted now. What he said has faded from the minds of men despite its enchanting, its enormous effect at the moment. On the other hand, the speech which is literature before it is spoken is ineffective or only partially effective at the moment, and if it is read afterwards, however much we may enjoy the essay, we never mistake it for the genuine eloquence of the spoken word. Macaulay is an example of this latter class, as Fox is of the former. Macaulay's speeches are essays, eloquent and rhetorical, but still essays; literature, and not speeches. He was listened to with interest and delight, but he was not a great parliamentary debater or speaker. The highest oratory, therefore, must combine in exact balance the living force and freshness of the spoken word with the literary qualities which alone ensure endurance. The best examples of this perfection are to be found in the world of imagination, in the two speeches of Brutus and Mark Antony in the play of Julius Cæsar. They are speeches and nothing else, — one cool, stately, reasonable; the other a passionate, revolutionary appeal, hot from the heart and pouring from the lips with unpremeditated art, and yet they both have the literary quality, absolutely supreme in this instance, because Shakespeare wrote them.

It is not the preparation or even the writing out beforehand, therefore, which makes a speech into an essay, for these things can both be done without detracting from the spontaneity, without dulling the sound of the voice which the wholly great speech must have, even on the printed page. The speech loses when the literary quality becomes predominant, and absolute success as high as it is rare comes only from the nice balance of the two essential ingredients. You find this balance, this combination, in Demosthenes and Isocrates, although I venture to think that those two great masters lean, if at all, too much to the literary side. In Cicero, although in matter and manner the best judges would rank him below the Greek masters, the combination is quite perfect. One of his most famous speeches, it is said, was never delivered at all, and none the less it is a speech and nothing else, instinct with life and yet with the impalpable literary feeling all through it, the perfect production of a very beautiful and subtle art. Among English orators Burke undoubtedly comes nearest to the union of the two qualities, and while the words of Fox and Pitt remain unread and unquoted, except by students, Burke's gorgeous sentences are recited and repeated by successive generations. Yet there is no doubt that Burke erred on the literary side, and we find the proof of it in the fact that he often spoke to empty benches, and that Goldsmith could say of him :

"Too deep for his hearers still went on refining,
And thought of convincing while they thought of dining."

Burke was a literary man as well as an orator and a statesman. Webster was not a literary man at all. He never wrote books or essays, although, in Dr. Johnson's phrase, he had literature and loved it. He was an orator, pure and simple ; his speeches, good, bad, or indifferent, are speeches — never essays or anything but speeches — and yet upon all alike is the literary touch. In all is the fine literary quality, always felt, never seen, ever present, never obtrusive. He had the combination of Shakespeare's Brutus or Antony, of Demosthenes or Cicero, and when he rose to his greatest heights he reached a place beyond the fear of rivalry.

Would you have a practical proof and exhibition

of this fact, turn to any serious and large debate
in Congress, and you will find Webster continually
quoted, as he is in every session, quoted twenty
times as often as any other public man in our history. He said many profound, many luminous, many
suggestive things; he was an authority on many
policies and on the interpretation of the Constitution. But there had been others of whom all this
might be said; there were kings before Agamemnon,
but they are rarely quoted, while Webster is quoted
constantly. He had strong competitors in his own
day and in his own field, able, acute, and brilliant
men. He rose superior to them, I think, in his lifetime, but now that they are all dead Webster is
familiar to hundreds to whom his rivals are little
more than names. So far as familiarity in the
mouths of men goes, it is Eclipse first and the rest
nowhere. It is the rare combination of speech and
literature; it is the literary quality, the literary
savor, which keeps what Webster said fresh, strong,
and living. When we open the volumes of his
speeches it is not like unrolling the wrappings of an
Egyptian mummy, to find within a dried and shriv-
elled form, a faint perfume alone surviving to recall
faintly the vanished days, as when

"Some queen, long dead, was young."

Rather it is like the opening of Charlemagne's tomb,
when his imperial successor started back before the

enthroned figure of the great emperor looking out upon him, instinct with life under the red glare of the torches.

Let us apply another and surer test. How many speeches to a jury in a criminal trial possessing neither political nor public interest survive in fresh remembrance seventy years after their delivery? I confess I can think of no jury speeches of any kind which stand this ordeal except, in a limited way, some speeches of Erskine, and those all have the advantage of historical significance, dealing as they do with constitutional and political questions of great moment. But there is one of Webster's speeches to a jury which lives to-day, and no more crucial test could be applied than the accomplishment of such a feat. The White murder case was simply a criminal trial, without a vestige of historical, political, or general public interest. Yet Webster's speech for the prosecution has been read and recited until wellnigh hackneyed. It is in readers and manuals, and is still declaimed by schoolboys. Some of its phrases are familiar quotations and have passed into general speech. Let me recall a single passage:

" He has done the murder. No eye has seen him; no ear has heard him. The secret is his own, and it is safe.

" Ah, gentlemen, that was a dreadful mistake. Such a secret can be safe nowhere. The whole creation of God has neither nook nor corner where the guilty can bestow it and say it is safe. . . . A thousand eyes turn at once to explore every man, everything, every circumstance connected with the time and place; a thousand ears catch every whisper; a thousand excited minds intensely dwell on the scene, shedding all their light, and ready to kindle the slightest circumstance into a blaze of discovery. Meantime the guilty soul cannot keep its own secret. It is false to itself; or, rather, it feels an irresistible impulse of conscience to be true to itself. It labors under its guilty possession, and knows not what to do with it. The human heart was not made for the residence of such an inhabitant. It finds itself preyed on by a torment which it dares not acknowledge to God or man. A vulture is devouring it, and it can ask no sympathy or assistance either from heaven or earth. The secret which the murderer possesses soon comes to possess him, and, like the evil spirits of which we read, it overcomes him and leads him whithersoever it will. He feels it beating at his heart, rising to his throat, and demanding disclosure. He thinks the whole world sees it in his face, reads it in his eyes, and almost hears its workings in the very silence of his thoughts. It has become his master. It betrays his discretion, it breaks down his courage, it conquers his prudence. When suspicions from without begin

to embarrass him and the net of circumstance to
entangle him, the fatal secret struggles with still
greater violence to burst forth.   It must be confessed ; it will be confessed.   There is no refuge
from confession but suicide, and suicide is confession."

Those are words spoken to men, not written for
them.   It is a speech and nothing else, and yet we
feel all through it the literary value and quality which
make it imperishable.   Take another example.   When
Webster stood one summer morning on the ramparts
of Quebec and heard the sound of drums and saw
the English troops on parade, the thought of England's vast world empire came strongly to his mind.
The thought was very natural under the circumstances, not at all remarkable nor in the least
original.   Some years later, in a speech in the Senate, he put his thought into words, and this, as
every one knows, is the way he did it : " A power
which has dotted over the surface of the whole
globe with her possessions and military posts, whose
morning drum-beat, following the sun and keeping
company with the hours, circles the earth with one
continuous and unbroken strain of the martial airs
of England."

The sentence has followed the drum-beat round
the world and has been repeated in England and in
the antipodes by men who never heard of Webster

and probably did not know that this splendid description of the British Empire was due to an
American. It is not the thought which has carried
these words so far through time and space. It is
the beauty of the imagery and the magic of the
style. Let me take one more very simple example
of the quality which distinguishes Webster's speeches
above those of others, which makes his words and
serious thoughts live on when others, equally weighty
and serious, perhaps, sleep or die. In his first
Bunker Hill oration he apostrophized the monument, just as any one else might have tried to do,
and this is what he said: "Let it rise, let it rise
till it meet the sun in his coming; let the earliest
light of morning gild it, and parting day linger and
play on its summit."

Here the thought is nothing, the style everything. No one can repeat those words and be deaf
to their music or insensible to the rhythm and
beauty of the prose with the Saxon words relieved
just sufficiently by the Latin derivatives. The ease
with which it is done may be due to training, but
the ability to do it comes from natural gifts which,
as Goethe says, "we value more as we get older
because they cannot be stuck on." Possibly to
some people it may seem very simple to utter such a
sentence as I have quoted. To them I can only
repeat what Scott says somewhere about Swift's

style, perhaps the purest and strongest we have in the language. " Swift's style," said Scott, " seems so simple that one would think any child might write like him, and yet if we try we find to our despair that it is impossible."

Such, then, were the qualities which in their perfect combination put Webster among the very few who stand forth as the world's greatest orators. In this age of ours when the tendency is to overpraise commonplace work, to mistake notoriety for fame and advertisement for reputation, it is of inestimable worth to a people to have as one of their own possessions such a master of speech, such a standard of distinction and of real excellence as we find in Webster. Such an orator deserves a statue.

But there is yet another ground, deeper and more serious than this. Webster deserves a statue for what he represented, for the message he delivered, and for that for which he still stands and will always stand before his countrymen and in the cold, clear light of history. He was born just at the end of the war of the Revolution, when the country was entering upon the period of disintegration and impotence known as that of the Confederation. He was too young to understand and to feel those bitter years of struggle and decline which culminated in the adoption of the Constitution. But the first impressions of his boyhood must have been of the prosperity, strength, and honor which came from the new instrument of government and from the better union of the States. His father followed his old chief in politics as he had in the field, and Webster grew up a Federalist, a supporter of Washington, Hamilton, and Adams, and of the leaders of their party. As he came to manhood he saw the first assault upon the national principle in the Virginia and Kentucky resolutions. He had entered public life when the second attack came in the movement which ended with the Hartford convention, and with which, New England Federalist as he was, he could feel no sympathy. Again fifteen years passed and the third assault was delivered in the nullification doctrines of South Carolina.

Webster was then at the zenith of his powers, and he came forward as the defender of the Constitution. In the reply to Hayne he reached the highest point in parliamentary oratory and left all rivals far behind. He argued his case with consummate skill, both legally and historically. But he did far more than this. He was not merely the great orator defending the Constitution, he was the champion of the national principle. Whether the Constitution was at the outset an experiment or not, whether it was a contract from which each or all of the signatories could withdraw at will, was secondary. The great fact was that the Constitution had done its work. It had made a nation. Webster stood forth in the Senate and before the country as the exponent of that fact and as the defender of the nation's life against the attacks of separatism. This was his message to his time. This was his true mission. In that cause he spoke as none had ever spoken before and with a splendor of eloquence and a force of argument to which no one else could attain.

It is not to be supposed for an instant that Webster discovered the fact that the Constitution had made a nation or that he first and alone proclaimed a new creed to an unthinking generation. His service was equally great, but widely different from this. The great mass of the American people felt dumbly, dimly perhaps, but none the less deeply and surely, that they had made a nation some day to be a great nation, and they meant to remain such and not sink into divided and petty republics. This profound feeling of the popular heart Webster not only represented, but put into words. No slight service this, if rightly considered; no little marvel this capacity to change thought into speech, to give expression to the feelings and hopes of a people and crystallize them forever in words fit for such a use. To this power, indeed, we owe a large part of the world's greatest literature. The myths and legends of Greece were of no one man's invention. They were children of the popular imaginings — vague, varying — floating hither and thither, like the mists of the mountains. But Homer touched them, and they started up into a beautiful, immortal life to delight and charm untold generations. Æschylus and Sophocles put them upon the stage, and they became types of the sorrows of humanity and of the struggle of man with fate. The Sagas of the far north, confused and diffuse but full of poetry and imagination, slumbered until the Minnesingers wove them into the Niebelungen Lied, and again until a great composer set them before our eyes, so that all men could see their beauty and pathos and read their deeper meanings. Sir Thomas Mallory rescued the Arthurian legends from chaos, and in our own day a great poet has turned them into forms which make their beauty clear to the world. Thus popular imaginings, dumb for the most part, finding at best only a rude expression, have been touched by the hand of genius and live forever.

So in politics Jefferson embodied in the Declaration of Independence the feelings of the American people and sounded to the world the first note in the great march of Democracy, which then began. The Marseillaise, in words and music, burned with the spirit of the French Revolution and inspired the armies which swept over Europe. Thus Webster gave form and expression, at once noble and moving, to the national sentiment of his people. In what he said men saw clearly what they themselves thought,

but which they could not express. That sentiment
grew and strengthened with every hour, when men
had only to repeat his words, in order to proclaim
the creed in which they believed; and after he was
dead Webster was heard again in the deep roar of the
Union guns from Sumter to Appomattox. His message, delivered as he alone could deliver it, was potent
in inspiring the American people to the terrible sacrifices by which they saved the nation when he slept
silent in his grave at Marshfield. Belief in the Union
and the Constitution, because they meant national
greatness and national life, was the great dominant
conviction of Webster's life. It was part of his temperament. He loved the outer world, the vast ex-
panses of sea and sky, all that was large and unfettered
in nature. So he admired great states and empires,
and had little faith in small ones, or in the happiness
or worth of a nation which has no history and which
fears its fate too much to put its fortune to the touch
when the accepted time has come.

It was not merely that as a statesman he saw the
misery and degradation which would come from the
breaking of the Union as well as the progressive
disintegration which was sure to follow, but the very
thought of it came home to him with the sharpness
of a personal grief which was almost agonizing.
When, in the 7th of March speech, he cried out,
"What States are to secede? What is to remain

American ? What am I to be ?" a political opponent said the tone of the last question made him shudder as if some dire calamity was at hand. The greatness of the United States filled his mind. He had not the length of days accorded to Lord Bathurst, but the angel of dreams had unrolled to him the future, and the vision was ever before his eyes.

This passionate love of his country, this dream of her future, inspired his greatest efforts, were even the chief cause at the end of his life of his readiness to make sacrifices of principle which would only have helped forward what he dreaded most, but which he believed would save that for which he cared most deeply. In a period when great forces were at work which in their inevitable conflict threatened the existence of the Union of States, Webster stands out above all others as the champion, as the very embodiment of the national life and the national faith. More than any other man of that time he called forth the sentiment more potent than all reasonings which saved the nation. It was a great work, greatly done, with all the resources of a powerful intellect and with an eloquence rarely heard among men. We may put aside all his other achievements, all his other claims to remembrance, and inscribe alone upon the base of his statue the words uttered in the Senate, " Liberty and Union, now and forever, one and inseparable." That single sentence recalls all the noble speeches which breathed only the greatness of the country and the prophetic vision which looked with undazzled gaze into a still greater future. No other words are wanted for a man who so represented and so expressed the faith and hopes of a nation. His statue needs no other explanation so long as the nation he served and the Union he loved shall last.

THREE GOVERNORS OF MASSACHUSETTS

I

FREDERIC T. GREENHALGE[1]

THE great mystery of death is always the same. Whether we behold it under " the canopies of costly state," or on the edge of a murky city river, where the body of some nameless outcast has been washed ashore, we bare our heads and bow in reverence before the poor piece of earth; yesterday humanity, to-day in its stillness the visible sign of that over-ruling Power which alike guides the universe and " doth the ravens feed, yea, providently caters for the sparrow."

Yet there are certain circumstances which heighten and sharpen the always solemn lesson of death. When a man is cut down in his prime, with all his natural force unabated and his power of mind and character still widening and strengthening, the blow

---

[1] Address delivered in Mechanics Hall, Boston, April 18, 1896, on the occasion of the public memorial service held by order of the Government of the State of Massachusetts in commemoration of the life and public services of Frederic T. Greenhalge, late Governor of the Commonwealth.

strikes us with peculiar keenness. When that man is also the actual representative of the sovereignty of the State, to whom have been given authority and command, and in whose hands has been placed the power to give or withhold liberty and life, his death touches the heart and the imagination alike, and the lesson of mortality sounds to us in louder and deeper tones than ever before. Then come home to us the familiar words of the Elizabethan dramatist :

> " The glories of our blood and state
> Are shadows, not substantial things ;
> There is no armor against fate ;
> Death lays his icy hand on kings."

Such has been the sad experience of Massachusetts within the last month. For the first time in seventy years, the psalmist's span of human life, the governor of the Commonwealth has died in office. He has died with all his honors thick upon him, in the meridian of his usefulness, beloved and respected by all conditions of men.

The office of governor has always meant a great deal to the people of Massachusetts. The early colonial tradition of the days when under a trading charter the Puritans built up an independent State has never been lost. That tradition taught men to hold in reverence the head of the State which embodied for them and for their fathers before them the great struggle for religious and political independence which had brought them to the wilderness. Never since that time has the governorship of the old State sunk in importance or come to occupy a secondary place in the political world. To be governor of Massachusetts has always been regarded by the people of the State as one of the highest honors to which a Massachusetts man could attain. The people of other States have sometimes jested at this sentiment of ours, but it is none the less noble and wise. It springs from the just State pride which we all feel, and has done much to give us the long line of distinguished men who have filled the high place of our chief magistrate. This sentiment in regard to the office encircles our governors with respect and honor while they live, and brings us in reverence and affection to mourn them when they are dead. Thus it is peculiarly fitting that the State should show to the memory of a governor who died at his post, faithful to the last, the honor in which his high office is held by all the people of the Commonwealth.

But there is another and still better reason than this for the grief of the State, for the action of the official representatives of the people and for these services here to-day. The governor, in virtue of his high place, is entitled to these honors, but the man himself has earned them by his public service, his character, and his career, — better titles to the respect and sorrow of Massachusetts than any which official distinction can ever give.

The old saying, " Speak naught but good of the dead," although sometimes abused and still oftener sneered at, is, nevertheless, like many other old sayings, founded on the broad and generous sense of mankind. Men who make their mark upon their time in any way, and especially public men, are certain to meet with abundance of censure and misunderstanding in the heated struggles of our active, energetic life. When they have passed into history, when Dr. Johnson's limit of the hundred years necessary to a right estimate has come and gone, the historian in his turn is sure to criticise them again with entire coolness, and let us hope with more justice than their contemporaries. It is only right, therefore, and it is necessary also to that final summing up of history, when friendship and enmity have alike paled their fires, that there should be a moment in which all that is best in a man's life and work should be set forth without deduction, free alike from the sharpness of the contemporary critic or the cold balancing of the future historian. Such a moment comes when we stand beside the hardly closed grave, and when grief and affection for the dead are uppermost in our hearts.

It is the fashion to call such utterances at such a time eulogy, which, after all, means merely the

good word; and it is also the fashion to think of
eulogy as in a large measure conventional and in-
sincere.   But this is, after all, a shallow and a
narrow view.   Rough manners do not necessarily
mean rugged honesty, although they are sometimes
employed to convey that idea.   Eulogy is more
likely to be true than invective, and good words than
bad.   Criticism has fallen so much into the evil
habit of mere fault-finding that it is generally understood to mean only hostile comment.   It is too often
forgotten that the true function of criticism is to
point out merits as well as defects, and that the
highest criticism is that which, unblinded by prejudice and fearless in its blame of error, shows to the
world what is best in a book or in a man.   Therefore we meet to-day not to utter the vain commonplaces of perfunctory praise in memory of a man
who loved truth and hated shams, but to speak of
him words at once good and true which love and
sorrow bring naturally to our lips.

The highest praise we can bestow upon any man
is to say that the story of his life, of what he said
and what he did, of what he was and how he took
part in the life of his time, is his best eulogy.   We
can say this truthfully of our dead governor, and
it is enough, for that simple statement is in itself
the full meed of honor.   It is in his life that I
have found his best eulogy, for there his own works

praise him better than any words of mine can possibly do.

Frederic Thomas Greenhalge was born in Clitheroe, county of Lancaster, England, July 19, 1842, the only son in a family of seven children of William and Jane (Slater) Greenhalge. The father, William Greenhalge, was the son of Thomas Greenhalg of Burnley. The latter was the son of John Greenhalg, who was the son of Thomas Greenhalg, attorney-at-law in Preston. The surname of the Lancaster family was apparently spelled without a final " e," and is thoroughly and characteristically English. William Greenhalge, the father of the governor, is described by those who knew him as a man of education, and possessed also of much artistic ability. Some of the pictures painted by him in early life are said to be still preserved in Edenfield, where the family lived for a time. About the year 1847 William Greenhalge joined his brother Thomas as a master engraver to calico printers, under the style of Greenhalge Bros., their works being situated at Stubbins bridge, between Rams Bottom and Edenfield. The business, however, did not prosper, and in May, 1855, William Greenhalge with his wife and family emigrated to America in order to improve his fortunes, and in pursuance of an engagement with the Merrimac Printing Company at Lowell to take the general management of the engraving department at a salary of four hundred pounds per annum, and an increase at the expiration of three years. The salary was a high one for those days, and it shows beyond all doubt that William Greenhalge was a man of training and artistic capacity, able to take control of the important department of design, upon which the success of print works so largely depends.

As soon as he had settled in his new position his children were sent to school, and his only son, who was evidently a precocious lad, early took high rank in his classes. In the high school at Lowell he is recalled as the leader of his class and the first winner of the Carney medal. He also showed, even at this early age, the taste for literature which accompanied him through life, by establishing a school review, edited and written by the boys, which I believe is still continued. As was to be expected, this eager, active-minded boy longed for the highest education, and in the fall of 1859, after the usual preparation, he entered Harvard College. His course there was not without distinction. At the close of his sophomore year he was elected orator of the " Institute of 1770," and subsequently became one of the editors of the old Harvard Magazine.

Love of learning brought him to Harvard through much hard work and many sacrifices. But he was not a mere bookworm. He had then, as always,

that sanest of qualities, — a great love for outdoor
air and outdoor sports. His fondness for sports,
indeed, resulted in an accident from which he suffered
for many years. Those were the days, not of the
football games which we know and which timid
people denounce, because now and then some one is
hurt, but of what were known as football fights, in
which there was very little football and a great deal
of fighting. The classes faced each other on the
Delta with the football between them, and fought.
It was a rough pastime, in which, in one form or
another, English-speaking boys have always indulged,
and which has done the race a great deal of good in
the long run. The Duke of Wellington, if the familiar
tradition may be believed, thought that the spirit it
bred helped him to win the battle of Waterloo. Greenhalge at all events went in with his fellows because
he was thoroughly brave and healthy-minded, and
loved to taste the delight of battle with his peers.
If he had not had that spirit he would not have been
the man he was, and it went with him through life.
He had the ill-luck to be one of those who were
seriously hurt. In a fall he injured his back and suffered much from it for some time afterwards, but he
never complained, and was always glad that he stood
up in the rough football fight just as he stood up in
later years with the same spirit in the greater battles
of professional and public life.

He loved his college life in all its phases, but he was not destined to complete his course at that time. His college career was suddenly interrupted by the death of his father in 1862, his junior year at Harvard, and the young student of twenty suddenly became the mainstay and sole support of his mother and six sisters. Like many another college boy brought sharply face to face with the hardest realities of life, Greenhalge found temporary employment as a school-teacher at Chelmsford. Subsequently he was employed in the American bolt shop at Lowell, but devoted all his spare time to the study of law in the office of Brown & Alger. While he was thus meeting the responsibilities thrust upon him, the nation was engaged in the mighty struggle of the Civil War. To this Mr. Greenhalge could not remain indifferent. He had become a thorough American. He hated slavery, and love of country was strong within him. So he put aside all private interests and determined to enter the army. Unfortunately, his physical condition at that time, owing to the accident in college, was not good, and the examining surgeon, to whom he presented himself, rejected him with the comment that there were enough " sick boys in the hospitals already." Greenhalge's action was characteristic of the man. Despite the medical verdict, he determined to go to the front, be the cost what it might. Accordingly, in October of 1863 he went to Newberne, N. C., and was there placed in the commissary department. When the city was attacked in February, 1864, he offered his services in the defence, and was given a command in a force of colored troops. While engaged in that duty he was stricken down with malarial fever, and after a few weeks' illness was sent home. This was his first glimpse of the South, to which a little more than thirty years later he was to return on another and far different errand, as the governor of Massachusetts, bearing a message of fraternity and good-will to a sister State. He had thrown his whole energy into the Union cause, and the result of his efforts was bitterly disappointing. There was a touch of pathos in the way he summed up his army experience. " I got," he says, "neither commission, pension, nor record, — nothing but malaria." Yet he deserved as much credit as men who got all three, for he gave all he could. He served wherever he could help his country, without a thought of self, and no man can do more.

After his recovery from the illness caused by his service in the Union army he renewed his law studies, and in 1865 he was admitted to the Middlesex bar, entering at once upon the practice of his profession. In 1870 he received from Harvard the degree of A.B. Two years later he married Miss Nesmith, daughter of Lieutenant-Governor John Nesmith, whose name

and family have been so long and honorably connected with the growth and upbuilding of Lowell
from the earliest days of the city. He was now
established in life. Happy in his home and his
marriage, devoted to his children, earnest in the
pursuit of his profession, he was also respected by
his fellow townsmen and popular in society, where
his charm of manner, his wit and humor, his clever-
ness as an amateur actor, were all appreciated.

Four years before his marriage he had taken his
first step in public life. In 1868 he was chosen to
the common council, and was re-elected the following
year. He also organized the Grant Campaign Club
in Lowell, and was its business manager. It has
been said that Mr. Greenhalge's friends found it
difficult at first to interest him in active politics,
although the larger public questions always absorbed
his attention. How true this may be I do not know,
but his aptitude for political affairs and his gift of
eloquent speech were unmistakable, and, once em-
barked in a political career, he soon became a leader
in municipal affairs. Such honors and responsibilities as the city could give came to him in varied
forms for wellnigh a score of years, and it is evident
that he early won and never lost a high place in the
esteem and affection of the people of Lowell. From
1871 to 1873 he was a member of the school board.
In 1874 he was made a special justice of the police

court at Lowell, and served for ten years, when he resigned. In 1879 he was brought forward as a candidate for mayor. This was done in the face of the opposition of many of the older politicians, who feared that he could not develop strength enough to beat his opponent, a popular Democratic leader. His friends thought otherwise, went vigorously to work, and carried Greenhalge delegates in four of the six wards. Events justified their wisdom and their belief in their candidate, for Mr. Greenhalge was elected by a handsome majority, and served during the years 1880 and 1881, showing the same independence of thought and action which were so characteristic of his whole career. During his term of office he presided at the memorial exercises held on the South Common in memory of President Garfield, and delivered upon that occasion an address which was much admired at the time, and which added to his growing reputation as a speaker. He also drafted the memorial resolutions adopted by the city council. In 1881 he was an unsuccessful candidate for State senator.

Three years later he was elected a delegate from the Lowell district to the Republican national convention at Chicago. It was there that I was first brought into close relations with him. I had known him before, but only slightly. At Chicago I came to know him well, and I have very seldom met any man who attracted me so strongly and so quickly. We were fighting a losing fight against the popular candidate, because we thought it our duty to do so. It was a trying position, and I was at once impressed by Mr. Greenhalge's good sense, by his modesty, his entire fearlessness, and his indifference to personal considerations. What most drew me to him was that quick sympathy which was his greatest charm, and which was enhanced by his sense of humor, the most sympathetic of all qualities. As is well known, we were beaten in the convention; but although the contest had been heated and even bitter, Mr. Greenhalge did not swerve or vary in his loyalty to his party, or in the fidelity which we believed simple honesty and good faith required us as delegates to show to the brilliant leader whom we had opposed and whom the convention nominated. As soon as he reached home Mr. Greenhalge at once made a strong speech in Lowell in support of Mr. Blaine and of the Republican party, whose principles and policies he believed essential to the welfare and prosperity of the country. As he began, so he went on, and gave generously, as he always did, of his time and strength to upholding and advocating the Republican cause.

In the year following the presidential election he was chosen one of the Lowell Representatives to the lower branch of the State legislature, where he did excellent service. He was elected, owing to his personal popularity, in a Democratic district, but was defeated for re-election by one vote. Upon the occasion of the semi-centennial of Lowell in 1886 he delivered the historical address, which added still further to his reputation as an orator. In 1888 he was chosen city solicitor.

His successful career in Lowell, together with his popularity, his services in the political campaigns, and his standing as a public speaker had already marked him for higher preferment, and as a man fit for a larger field of action. The presidential campaign of 1888 at last brought the opportunity, and his party in the district turned to him as their candidate for Congress. The fight which followed his nomination was a stubborn one, but he made an aggressive and effective canvass, and was elected by a handsome plurality.

When he resigned his office as city solicitor in 1889 to go to Washington, the first period of his life closed. He was now to enter upon the broader field of national politics, and he came to it at a time of great stress and excitement. The Fifty-first Congress was not a peaceful one. It was the second Republican Congress since the days of Grant, and the party majority hung by a slender thread. There was a great work to be done, nothing less than the reform of the rules and the restoration to the majority of its rights and responsibilities. The opening days of the session were marked by much turbulence, and all the known tactics of obstructive parliamentary warfare were resorted to by a resolute and defiant opposition. It was a time which demanded the best resources of trained and experienced leadership, and there seemed to be but a slight opening for a new and untried man. When the House organized and the committees were announced, Mr. Greenhalge found himself placed on the committees on elections, revision of the laws, and reform in the civil service. To the first of these committees was intrusted the important function of hearing and deciding contests for seats, of which there was an unusually large number in that Congress, most of them coming from Southern States. Party feeling ran high, and the debates which followed the various reports on election cases provoked great partisan bitterness. To the work of this committee Mr. Greenhalge devoted himself with his accustomed energy and ability.

The first case to be called up was that of Smith v. Jackson, from West Virginia. During this debate Mr. Greenhalge made his maiden speech. The occasion could not have been more happily selected. The House was crowded, and the interest was keen. His analysis of the legal points involved was lucid and convincing, and the whole speech was tinged with

a delicious satire which caught the House at once.
At the close he was accorded hearty and enthusiastic
applause. The House recognized immediately that
he was a sound lawyer, a brilliant speaker, and a
strong debater, and the opinion of the House on
these points is of the best, and is not easily won.
It was a triumph for a first speech. Henceforth
his place was secure, and he became at once one of
the leaders of the House. His reputation thus made,
he found himself beset by every contestant with
demands for assistance. These appeals he found
it difficult to resist, and he did much effective work
in placing these election controversies before the
House. The amount of labor involved in sifting
evidence in each case was immense, but the reward
came in the form of an established legal and forensic
reputation. It is impossible to do more than allude
to perhaps his most eloquent effort while a member
of the House, the speech made in the Waddill v.
Wise Case. Edmund Waddill, Jr., the Republican
candidate, contested the seat of his Democratic opponent, who had been given the certificate of election
from one of the Virginia districts. It was clearly
shown in the evidence that in three precincts of one
ward in the city of Richmond long lines of colored
voters had remained standing in front of the election
booths throughout the night before election and during the entire election day until the polls were closed,

in the vain hope of being allowed to cast their
ballots. The whole question of the right to the
seat turned upon whether these ballots should be
counted. In the course of his speech Mr. Greenhalge said:

"Shall the law be ineffectual? Shall the whole
majesty of the law stand silent, powerless, inactive
as yonder obelisk, or shall that law be clothed with
power and strength enough to give to every man in
that colored line the same rights that the white
millionaire has? Mr. Speaker, I have heard and
read with admiration of that memorable thin, red
line which repelled the fiery onset of Napoleon at
Waterloo; but I say that this thin, black line, standing from sunrise to sunset in Jackson ward, means
as much for human freedom and civil liberty as the
memorable thin, red line at Waterloo. I go further,
Mr. Speaker: I say that if this House does not do
justice to every man in those lines in the first, third,
and fourth precincts of Jackson ward, in the city of
Richmond, and count every vote there legally tendered, then the flaming lines of Gettysburg were
nothing more than a vain and empty show, and even
the grand words of Lincoln, spoken over the graves
of Gettysburg, become only as 'sounding brass and
tinkling cymbals.'"

The wave of popular discontent which engulfed
the party in power in 1890 carried Mr. Greenhalge

down with it, despite his personal popularity, and owing to his neglect of his own interests by going out of his district to give generous aid to other Republicans. He made a gallant fight, but was defeated by about four hundred and fifty votes. If his disappointment was acute at thus finding himself unexpectedly thrust back on the threshold of a brilliant congressional career, no sign of it escaped him. He returned cheerfully to the practice of his profession, and there is no doubt that for a time he regarded his public life as closed. As early as April, 1892, in a letter to the chairman of the congressional committee, he declined to have his name considered as a candidate for Congress in the approaching canvas.

The unlooked-for and accidental defeat of the Republican nominee for governor in 1892 made the selection of a new candidate probable in the succeeding year. Several gentlemen were put forward, and during the summer months of 1893 a friendly and earnest contest was waged for the nomination. Some time before the convention assembled, however, it became apparent that Mr. Greenhalge was the popular choice, and the other candidates withdrew. The incidents of the campaign that followed are still fresh in the public mind. After a canvas of great brilliancy, Mr. Greenhalge was triumphantly elected, thus restoring the line of Republican governors, which had been broken for the longest period in the history of the party since it had been dominant in Massachusetts, and on January 4, 1894, he was inaugurated. In the fall of 1894 and again in 1895 he was re-elected by heavy majorities, the largest which had been cast for any governor in almost a generation. When he first received the nomination, he told the convention that he accepted it as the greatest responsibility of his life, and his subsequent career showed that this feeling never left him for an instant. Throughout his administration he did his duty as he conceived it, without regard to his personal interests or to the effect of his acts upon his own political fortunes. He may have made mistakes; every successful man who does things worth doing is sure to err at times, and he would have been the last man to claim infallibility, for he was too human and too manly; but he never acted from a mean or low motive, and he had a quick and sound judgment. He decided each question as it was presented to him independently and fearlessly, not infrequently against the advice and judgment of some of his warm supporters.

He had entire courage, physical and moral. Early in his first term a mob entered the State House. They had done no harm, but they were in that uncontrolled condition when serious danger was likely to spring up in an instant. A mass of human beings stricken with panic or gathered in a mob, excited and leaderless, is always a peril. When the governor heard that this crowd was in the State House and menacing the legislature, he did not stop to consider what should be done, but went out at once and looked disorder so squarely in the face that quiet was restored. This was the quick instinct of the high-spirited man, when the sudden pressure comes, — the two-o'clock-in-the-morning courage which Napoleon admired. Governor Greenhalge sent no one; he went himself to meet the peril, if there was one, and at his coming the danger faded and fled.

Courage of a different kind he had also, — that moral courage which makes a decision among conflicting interests, and after careful consideration, as he showed on various occasions. He did not shrink from putting his veto upon a measure which had a powerful interest or a popular cry behind it, whenever he thought his duty to the State required it; the State sustained him, and even the people, whom he disappointed, in the end respected and trusted him more. He was not opinionated, but for none of his more important acts, when he came to review them dispassionately, did he experience any regret. He was justly conscious of his purity of motive, and the apologetic attitude was one he never assumed. A conspicuous instance of this trait appeared the last time he faced a Republican convention. He alluded to several strictures which had

been passed upon him, and then with an outburst of
deep feeling he closed a brief reference to his course
in office by saying to the delegates who had just
nominated him for the third term, "In the language
of the great reformer, so help me God, I could not do
otherwise."

He was diligent and industrious in his daily work,
and never shirked details.   With the growth of the
State the labors of the Executive have multiplied,
and Governor Greenhalge discharged them all con-
scientiously and faithfully.   The work now incident
to the office, the work really due to the public, is
enough to tax sufficiently the strength and ability of
any man.   But insensibly there has grown up the
habit of expecting the governor of Massachusetts to
be present and to speak at all sorts of gatherings
and on all kinds of occasions, wholly unofficial and
in no sense properly pertaining to the office.   These
incessant demands Governor Greenhalge met with
the generosity which was so marked a quality of his
character.   But the demands ought never to have
been made or complied with, for they put upon
him such a burden and so strained both body and
mind that at last his health gave way.   At first the
illness seemed trifling.   Then with a terrible shock
we heard that he was dying, and in a few days the
end came.   He died in his prime, worn out in the
public service, and the people of a great American

Commonwealth watched with loving sympathy over his last hours, and mourned beside his grave, near the busy city which he loved, and to which he had come, a little boy of English birth, forty years before.

So this honorable life of work and conflict, of happiness and success, closed. The first thought that comes to me as I look back over the record, is the strong race quality shown by Governor Greenhalge. He was born in England. He was of ancient English stock, formed by the mingling of Saxon and Dane many years before the "galloping Norman came." He was thirteen years old when he came to Lowell, and all the strong associations of his childhood belonged to England. Yet no better, no more thorough American ever lived than he. There was no foreign prefix and no hyphen attached to his Americanism. He received his education here; he absorbed the spirit of our life ; he was full of patriotism; he was for America against the world. The fact is, he came from the old home of the English-speaking people, to find here the larger part of that people as it exists to-day ; and in both branches the great race qualities, forged and welded through more than a thousand years of toil and strife, are the same. The differences are superficial, the identities profound. To a man like Governor Greenhalge, the ideas, the beliefs, the habits, the aspirations of the great American democracy appealed more strongly than those of the land he had left. The air of America was more native to him than that of the country of his birth. So he became and lived and died an American in every fibre of his being, something always worthy of remembrance among a people proud of their country and believing in its destiny.

One reason for his Americanism was that he was democratic in the true sense, cringing to no man, courteous to all. He was simple in his life, devoted and tender to wife and children, a lover of home, — the altar and shrine of the race who read the Bible in the language of Shakespeare. He was brave and loyal, — loyal with that chivalrous loyalty which is not too common, but which leads a man like him to come unasked to the aid of a friend, and to give and take blows in a friend's behalf, as the Black Knight came to the side of Ivanhoe when he was sore beset.

He was honest in word and deed, and untouched by the unwholesome passion for mere money, which is one of the darkest perils of these modern times. He loved literature and books with a real love and reverence, and held scholarship in honor, as it has always been held in New England, and I trust ever will be.

Of his qualities and gifts as a public man there is little need for me to speak. They are known to you all, and are fresh in your remembrance. The echoes of that ready speech, now flashing with humor and satire, now rich in eloquence and feeling, in imagery and allusion, still sound in our ears. With memory sharpened by sorrow, we all recall his ability in administration, his capacity for business, his unfailing charm of manner, his simple but strong religious faith, and his large and generous tolerance. These qualities were known and honored of all men, and they had their reward, not in the high offices which came to him, but in the confidence and affection which he inspired.

His was a life worth living. He made it so both for himself and for others. He did a man's work, he fought a man's fight, he made his mark upon his time. It is a life worth studying, not merely because it was an example of the rise from small beginnings to great conclusions, which it is one of the glories of our country to make possible for all men, but because it was a life of lofty aims, of high hopes, of honorable achievement. He has left us a fine and gracious memory, to be treasured in the history of the old State he served so well; and let this thought mingle with our sadness and linger longest in our memories. Let us end as we began, with the Elizabethan poet, no longer stern, but in a softer, tenderer strain. Let us not forget that if

"The garlands wither on our brow,"

it is also true that

"The actions of the just
Smell sweet and blossom in the dust."

THREE GOVERNORS OF MASSACHUSETTS

II

GEORGE D. ROBINSON [1]

YESTERDAY we had a memorial service in Boston for our Governor who had died in office. To-day we meet to do like honor to one of his near predecessors. The quick succession of these solemn observances is a sad reminder of the loss which has within a few months befallen the Commonwealth in the sudden death of two of her most trusted and eminent public men. Both deserved well of the Republic, both had done the State high service, both had lived lives and shown qualities which were an honor to Massachusetts.

He whose memory we would recall, and whose life and deeds we would praise here to-day, had withdrawn himself some years ago from the public career in which he had played such a distinguished part. He had returned to the active and successful

---

[1] An address delivered at a meeting in memory of George Dexter Robinson, Governor of Massachusetts, 1884–1887, held in Lexington, Massachusetts, his native town, on the one hundred and twenty-first anniversary of the battle with the British at that place.

pursuit of his profession, where he held a deservedly high position. He was cut down suddenly in the fulness of his strength, both of body and mind; and the news of his death brought deep sorrow to all the people of the State. His loss was as keenly felt as if he had still held office; for, although he had retired from public life, the services he had rendered, his high reputation, and his strong character made him in any sphere or in any field of human activity a potent influence and a pillar of strength to the community in which he lived.

There is a peculiar fitness in coming here on this day to honor his memory. Not only is this the town of his birth, but it is a famous and historic spot. Lexington is a name known to all Americans. When we tell the story of the long, brave struggle which made us an independent nation, we begin it here where for the first time the minute-men faced the soldiers of England. With it are entwined all the memories of the Revolution. It was to Lexington and Concord and Bunker Hill that Daniel Webster pointed first when he numbered the glories of Massachusetts. Here the memories dearest to our hearts awaken, and they are all American. They speak of American liberty, American courage, American union and independence. There is no jarring note anywhere. Hence the peculiar fitness of which I have spoken in our coming here to com-

memorate the life and services of Governor Robinson ;
for he was not only a distinguished man, but he was
a typical one.

He was a true son of the soil, an American, a New
Englander. Here the Puritans settled, here they
lived for generations, here their descendants fought
the first fight of the Revolution ; and here, if anywhere, in this historic American town we can learn
from the life of one of its children what the result
has been of the beliefs, the strivings, the traditions,
of the people who founded and built up New England, and in the course of the centuries have pushed
their way across the continent. In the career and
the character of Governor Robinson we have an
open book, where we can read a story which will
tell us what kind of man the civilization of the
English Puritans has been able to produce in this
nineteenth century, after so many years of growth
and battle in the New World. Has the result been
worthy of the effort and the struggle ? Has the race
advanced and grown stronger here under new influences in its two hundred and fifty years of American existence, or has it faltered, failed, and declined ?
These are questions of deep moment to us, children
of New England and Massachusetts. Let us turn
to the life of the man whose memory brings us here
to-day, and find the answer there.

One of the earliest of the Puritan settlements was

at Cambridge; and there a town sprang up with its
church and school-house, and in a short time with
the little college which has grown since then into
the great university we know to-day. As the years
went by, more and more land was taken up; and a
new settlement was formed to the north of the
college town, and known as Cambridge Farms.
Thither about 1706 came Jonathan Robinson with
his young wife, Ruth. He was born in 1682, the
son of William Robinson, of Cambridge, was a weaver
by trade, and moved from his birthplace that he
might get a farm and establish a home for his
family. He became one of the leading men of the
little settlement, was chosen a tythingman in 1735,
and in 1744 was one of the committee appointed
to " dignify and seat ye meeting-house," an important
social function in the early days of New England.

He had six children. The eldest, Jonathan, born
in 1707, married in his turn, and had a son named
Jacob, born in 1739. His son, also named Jacob, the
great-grandson of the Cambridge weaver, was born
in 1762. He lived to a great age, and was in his
turn a leader in the town, being selectman in 1805
and 1806, and for several years assessor. He had
nine children, among them Hannah, who became the
wife of Charles Tufts, the founder of Tufts College,
and Charles, the father of George D. Robinson, the
future governor, who was born January 20, 1834.

The mother of Governor Robinson was Mary Davis, of Concord, a lineal descendant of Dolor Davis, one of the earliest of the Plymouth settlers, and the ancestor of three Massachusetts governors. The mother of Mrs. Robinson was the daughter of Joseph Hosmer, who acted as adjutant in the fight at Concord Bridge.

I have traced this pedigree in some detail, not because it is remarkable, but because it is typical. It is characteristic of New England, and represents the rank and file — the yeomanry of Massachusetts — who have made the State and done so much to build the nation. How plainly they come before us, — these men and women of the unmixed Puritan stock! They were a simple, hard-working folk, tilling the ground, weaving their linen, bringing up their children in the fear of God, governing themselves, filling in their turn the town offices ; while they never lost their hold on higher things, respecting and seeking education, deeply religious, and with an abiding love of home and country. One of the Robinson name was in Captain Parker's company on the 19th of April at Lexington, and on the mother's side we find one of the officers at Concord. These Puritans came here at the outset to hear a sermon after their own fashion. They were stern and often intolerant, but always strong, determined men. As the generations passed, each doing its simple duty in thorough manner, the Puritan severity softened and mellowed; but the great qualities of the race remained unchanged, and never failed in war or peace.

From such ancestry did George Robinson come, and such were the traditions he inherited. His father was a farmer, a man respected in the town, of which he was many times selectman. The boy was brought up to the hard but vigorous life of a New England country town. His father's farm lay some two miles to the north of Lexington, in what was then a somewhat secluded spot. Here the boy soon began to bear his share of the responsibilities, and to help in the support of the family. There was a great deal of hard work on the farm, few leisure hours, not many books to read, and, as the nearest neighbor was nearly half a mile away, not much society. But among the New Englanders, as among the lowland Scotch, the two branches of the English-speaking race which have perhaps contended with harder conditions than any others, there was an ardent love of learning and a belief in the power and the value of education, for which no sacrifice was deemed too great.

So, while George Robinson helped his father on the farm, he managed to attend the district school for three or four months in the year. He did well at school, and one who knew him all his life says of him: "What he was as a man, he was as a boy, —

truthful, sincere, kind, and clean, — a boy whom every one respected and esteemed, making friends wherever he went." The means at the command of his family were so slender that he put aside the idea of ever getting to college; but, toward the close of his career in the more advanced schools, his teachers, who had a high opinion of his capacity, persuaded him to take the Harvard examinations. He passed successfully, and entered college in 1852. It was a hard struggle, and required many sacrifices. He went back and forth every day from his home in Lexington to his recitations in Cambridge. He lived on a pittance, earned money by teaching school, and by his rigid economy and self-denial completed his college course, and was graduated with his class in 1856. He took good rank at Harvard, graduating high enough to win a place in the Phi Beta Kappa. He was popular in his class, and a member of several societies. One of his classmates, Judge Smith, says of him: " Whatever he undertook, he did well and so thoroughly that he did not have to go over it a second time. I should say that he never hurried, and yet was always upon time. I do not believe he ever lost any time or strength in worrying. He did his best, and then calmly awaited results."

Thus he found himself face to face with the world at the age of twenty-two, with no capital except his education, his good brains, and his determined will.

His plan at that time seems to have been to study medicine; but, for immediate support, he took to teaching, obtaining a position as principal of the Chicopee High School, where he remained for nine years. During this period he seems to have kept up his studies of medicine. Meantime, on November 24, 1859, he had married; but in 1864 his wife died, and he soon after returned to his father's house, bringing with him his only child, a boy of four years. It was at this time that he changed his plans, and began the serious study of the law in the office of his brother. In 1866 he was admitted to the bar, ten years after his graduation. He was thirty-two years of age, and had come very late to the opening of his professional career. Once started, however, he made rapid progress. He returned to Chicopee, and opened an office in Cabot Hall Block on Market Square, a place which he retained until his comparatively recent removal to Springfield. The thoroughness and painstaking care with which he prepared his cases soon brought him a lucrative practice in a community where he was already so well known and so favorably regarded. Soon after he had established himself in his profession, on July 11, 1867, he again married, his second wife being the daughter of Joseph F. Simonds, of Lexington.

He had always taken an interest in all public questions; but as he had been late in coming to the bar, so he was slow in engaging in active politics. His public career began with his election to the lower branch of the legislature as the representative from Chicopee in the fall of 1874. He was at that time forty years of age, and accepted the office with genuine reluctance. In his one year of service in the House he was placed on the Judiciary Committee, serving on that committee side by side with Richard Olney, Chief Justice Mason of the Superior Court, the late William W. Rice, John Quincy Adams, and Congressman William S. Knox. The next year he went to the State Senate, where he also served one term, as he had done in the lower branch. During his two years of experience in the State legislature he quickly took high rank as a debater, and showed qualifications for public life which marked him for larger opportunities. They were not long in coming. In the fall of 1876 he was nominated as the Republican candidate for Congress in the old Eleventh District, so long and ably represented by Henry L. Dawes, which two years before had been carried by Chester W. Chapin, the Democratic nominee, by a plurality of nearly 6,000. Mr. Robinson took the stump at once, and after a vigorous struggle overcame the large adverse majority, and was elected to the Forty-fifth Congress by a plurality of 2,162. He was successively re-elected, without serious opposition, to the Forty-sixth, Forty-seventh, and Forty-eighth Congresses.

He brought to his new duties in Congress the trained habits of a student of political affairs, boldness in debate, ingenuity, resource, and a power of forcible and lucid statement, which soon commanded the attention of the House. Before the expiration of his first session his close attention to the duties of his position both in the committee room and on the floor of the House made the late Speaker Randall, a good judge of men, predict a distinguished future for the new member from Massachusetts. During his Congressional service he was given various important committee assignments, including places on the Judiciary Committee and on the Committee upon the Improvement of the Mississippi River. Mr. Robinson was regular in attendance upon the sessions of the House, and devoted his whole strength to the public business. During the second session of the Forty-fifth Congress he began to participate actively in the Congressional debates. As a debater, he was distinguished by incisiveness of speech and precision of statement, — qualities which made him a formidable antagonist. His familiarity with the rules also made him an authority in questions of parliamentary procedure, and he was frequently called to preside over a Democratic House.

In the fall of 1882 Mr. Robinson was elected for a fourth term, this time as the representative from the then new Twelfth District. His place in Congress was now an influential one; and he had come to be recognized as one of the leaders of the New England delegation and one of the strong men of the House. Back of him was a united and admiring constituency. His Congressional career seemed likely to be a long and eminent one; but it was suddenly terminated by the unanimous demand of his party to lead them in the fiercest campaign they had ever been called upon to make for victory in the State of Massachusetts.

In 1882 General Butler, supported by the whole Democratic party, and by a considerable number of Republicans, who constituted his personal following, had carried the State, and been elected Governor. His administration, by the course he chose to follow, had aroused deep resentments, and to the intense desire of the Republicans as a party to regain the State was added a great deal of personal bitterness. The Republican organization therefore began its work early, for there was much to do. But the all-important point to be decided was who should be the candidate to lead the fight against General Butler. It was neither an easy nor an inviting task, and the prospect of victory was anything but certain.

It was my fortune to be at that time chairman of the Republican State Committee, and in charge of the campaign. I had no personal acquaintance with Governor Robinson, and knew him only by reputation as a distinguished and leading member of Congress. It seemed to me, however, at the very start, on looking over the whole field, that he would be our strongest candidate against General Butler; but I felt that, in view of the serious contest before us, the candidate should be selected by the well-considered opinion of the party, and that it was not the time for any interference by the State Committee in regard to the nomination. I was, therefore, very careful to say nothing whatever as to my own views in regard to candidates. As time went on, several distinguished Republicans were suggested for the nomination; but in each case a refusal to run followed. Finally, party opinion settled down on Mr. Henry L. Pierce; and, as the date fixed for the convention approached, it was clear that he would be nominated with practical unanimity. That this would be the result of the convention was generally understood, and was accepted on all sides.

On the day before the convention Mr. Pierce sent for me, and told me that he could not be a candidate. His sudden withdrawal at the last moment was a very serious matter, when the all-important question of the nomination was thought to have been conclusively settled. It threatened to throw everything into confusion, and start us most unfortunately in the severe struggle which we knew was at hand. I remember very well the consternation of every one when I went back to the rooms of the State Committee, and stated officially that Mr. Pierce had finally withdrawn. I felt anxious myself, but not so much disturbed as the others; for I knew Mr. Robinson was coming to town, and I meant to appeal to him to step into the gap and take the nomination. I met him that day at the office of his brother, Charles Robinson, in the Rogers Building. Our interview is one of the incidents of my life which I most vividly remember. After we had shaken hands, I said to him, " Mr. Robinson, Mr. Pierce has withdrawn, and you must take the nomination." He looked at me with his head up in the confident manner so characteristic of him, and with which I became afterwards so familiar, and said, " Mr. Lodge, I have not sought the governorship; but, if the party wants me and needs me, I will stand." I shall never forget the relief which I felt and the confidence with which his answer, coming as it did in the midst of refusals and hesitations, inspired me.

He was nominated the next day, practically without opposition; and his short speech of acceptance gave to the convention the same feeling of confidence which he had already given to me. When he looked the delegates, as he did every one, squarely in the face, and said, " It is your duty to command : I count it mine to obey," a sense of relief filled the convention. After the days of doubt, hesitation, and alarm the strong man, the man able and willing to lead, had come; and every one recognized it. As we walked away together after the convention, he said to me : " We have a hard fight before us, and you and I are to be thrown together very closely. I want you to be perfectly frank with me about every- thing, and to call upon me unhesitatingly for all I can do. I am a poor man, and have no money to put into the campaign ; but my time and strength are at the service of the party." Every one knows how he kept his word ; but no one can appreciate it, I think, quite so fully as I do. The relations be- tween the chairman of a State committee and his candidate are not always very easy. The chairman, working for party victory, is obliged to press the candidate pretty hard, and sometimes almost un- reasonably ; but in that campaign the candidate met every demand upon him, not only willingly, but gladly.

Governor Robinson shrank from no effort and no fatigue. He made during the campaign, as I re- member, some seventy-three speeches. I think he made nine on the last day ; and he never failed in the force, variety, and freshness of what he said. With the exception of the Lincoln and Douglas de- bate, I do not believe that Governor Robinson's campaign against General Butler has ever been surpassed in a debate before the people. It was a close, hard fight; and I have never questioned that it was his commanding leadership which turned the scale. He never lost his temper, his good sense never failed. He followed his antagonist relentlessly, and without a syllable of personal abuse struck blow after blow, and never left an argument unanswered or a position unassailed. The confidence and enthusiasm which he inspired grew and strengthened with each day and with every speech; and when it was all over and the polls had closed, he received the news of his victory with the same calm cheerfulness with which he had faced the heady currents of the fight.

After his brilliant and successful campaign for the governorship, he went to Washington in December, 1883, to participate in the organization of the Forty-eighth Congress, to which he had been elected the year before. On the 2d of January following he forwarded his resignation of his seat in Congress to Governor Butler. The Governor's reply was characteristic: "Your resignation of your office of representative in the Forty-eighth Congress of the United States from the Twelfth District of Massachusetts, tendered to the Governor of the Commonwealth this morning, is hereby accepted, the reason prompting the same being so entirely satisfactory to the majority of the people of the State."

Thus he passed from the parliamentary field, for

which he was so peculiarly fitted, and where he had won so much success, to the high executive office of Governor of Massachusetts. He was twice re-elected without really serious opposition, and was never in danger of defeat. To the important business of administration he brought the same diligence, ability, thoroughness, and conscientious work which had marked his whole career. He was an extremely successful governor. He had entire courage, and never hesitated to stop a measure with his veto if he thought it wrong, no matter how strong the popular feeling in its favor appeared to be. He devoted to the endless details of executive business the same attention, thought, and ability which he used to give to an exciting debate in the national House, when he was speaking and voting with the eyes of the country upon him. He came up to the high standard which the State demands of her governors, and at the close of his last term he commanded the approval of all the people to a degree which is rarely witnessed. The State was proud of him, the people admired him; but the feeling which he inspired above all others was complete confidence in his ability, courage, and strength.

When he left the governorship, he returned to private life and to the practice of his profession. He liked the work of public life, as every strong man likes to do that which he knows he does well;

but Governor Robinson felt that his duty to his
family required him to abandon politics, although he
might have had anything the State could give,
and address himself to labors which would make
provision for the future and for those dearest to him.
There were no repinings and no rejoicings. He went
out of public life, leaving behind him all its attrac-
tion and all its drawbacks, with the same philo-
sophic cheerfulness with which he had accepted his
first nomination for governor or heard later the
news of his great victory flashed over the wires to
Chicopee. Once out of politics, he cast no backward
looks, but gave his whole strength to his profession,
although he would always come forward in the campaigns and help his party with a speech, when the
fight was hottest and his aid most needed.

Of his success at the bar, after his return to it
there is no need to speak. It is still fresh in every
one's mind. Thus busily engaged, nine years went
by; and then he was suddenly stricken down. He
was so strong, so temperate, so vigorous in all ways
that the idea of illness seemed utterly remote from
him. We all, I think, regarded him as a man, above
all others, who was destined to a long life and to a
strong old age, surpassing even that of his long-lived
ancestry. Death is the commonest of events; but
it is always a surprise, and in this case the shock was
especially sudden and severe. The blow was instant

and decisive, like the strong man who fell beneath it; but it was none the less hard to bear for the people of this Commonwealth, who had looked up to him, followed him, honored him. Still in his prime, in the vigor of his manhood, he had been reft from us; and the people of Massachusetts mourned beside his grave.

So the story of the life and the career ends with the sad ending of all our little human histories. It seems to me a very fine story, even when told as imperfectly and incompletely as I have told it to you. It is not only a life which it will be a pride to his children to recall, but it is full of meaning and encouragement to us all. The character and qualities of the man himself seem to me to shine out very brightly through the brief abstract and chronicle of what he did in this busy world. They are worth considering by all men who love Massachusetts, and who are inspired with eager, earnest hopes for the destiny of their country and their race.

Note, first, that he was a strong man physically, big, deep-chested, able to withstand toil and stress. This is a point which is too often overlooked; and yet it is of grave importance, for the puny races of men go to the wall. Governor Robinson was a fine proof of the fact that the descendants of the hardy Englishmen who settled here had not degenerated, but rather had waxed stronger in bone and muscle and sinews in their two hundred and fifty years of American life. Mind and character matched the physical attributes. Strength of will and vigor of mind were his two most characteristic qualities. He was exceedingly temperate in all ways, a man of pure, clean, wholesome life. The desires of the senses were under as much control as his temper. He was always cool, and his judgment was never clouded by excitement. The stern spirit of self-sacrifice to a great purpose, which brought the Puritans to the wilderness, survived in him, mellowed no doubt, but just as effective as of old in the conditions of life which he was called to meet. He had deep convictions on all questions; but he was always just, tolerant, and fair. He was a hard worker, one who never shirked and never complained. Rarely have I met a man of such even cheerfulness under all circumstances. The words which Washington used about the Constitution often came to my mind when I watched Governor Robinson's method of dealing with public affairs: "We have set up a standard to which the good and wise may repair: the event is in the hands of God." He did his best always, and never worried before nor repined after the event, if things went ill, nor rejoiced unduly, if they went well.

He made his greatest reputation as a debater in Congress and before the people. He was not a rhetorician, and never tried to be. When Antony says,

"I am no orator, as Brutus is ;
But, as you know me all, a plain, blunt man,
That love my friend.
I only speak right on,"

we recognize the artistic self-depreciation of the most consummate orator who ever lived, if he spoke as Shakespeare makes him speak. But what Antony said for effect might be said with truth of Governor Robinson. He was the plain, blunt man who spoke right on ; and he was a master of this most difficult and very telling kind of oratory. He was no phrase-maker, no rounder of periods, no seeker for metaphors ; but he was one of the most effective and convincing speakers, whether to Congress, to a great popular audience, or to a jury, that I ever listened to. The very way in which he faced an audience, with his head up, and a bold, confident, but never arrogant manner, calmed the most hostile and roused the most indifferent. He used simple language and clear sentences. He had a remarkable power of nervous, lucid statement, — a very great gift. His arguments were keen and well knit, and illumined by a strong sense of humor and a dry wit which were very delightful. He had, above all, the rare and most precious faculty of making his hearers feel that he was putting into words just what they had always thought, but had never been able to express quite so well. To do this is very difficult.

It does not come merely by nature. The most famous poet of Queen Anne's day thought it a very
great art; for he tells us that

"True wit is nature to advantage dressed;
What oft was thought, but ne'er so well expressed."

Governor Robinson was, in one word, a great
debater, — one of the best of his generation; and
when I say this, it implies that he was a man of unusual powers of thought, incisive, quick, and of large
mental resource.

But his remarkable ability as a speaker, his shrewd-
ness and justice and diligence in all the affairs of life,
his calm temper and his cheerful philosophy, while
they were all potent factors in his success and his
popularity, were not his only nor his highest qualities. It is a very happy thing to be popular and
successful; but it is a much nobler thing to command
the affectionate and deep confidence, not only of
friends, but of a great community. This Governor
Robinson did in a high degree, and the secret lay in
his character. People trusted him, not because he
was a brilliant and convincing speaker, of whom
they were proud, or even because he was a faithful
and admirable chief magistrate, but because they
knew him to be an entirely honest and fearless
man. They saw that he was simple in his life,
thoroughly democratic, educated, and trained, with

a mind open to new ideas, and yet with the ingrained conservatism and the reverence for law and order which New England has always cherished ; and, therefore, they believed in him. Instinctively, the people turned to him as the strong man fit for leadership and command, who would never waver in the face of danger and never betray a trust.

Is not our question as to the result of the Puritan civilization answered by such a life and such a character ? The old qualities are all there, the old fighting qualities, and ever with them the mastering sense of duty to God, to country, and to family. They have not weakened in the centuries that have come and gone. They have broadened, but they have not pined or faded. They have not been refined and cultivated to nothingness ; and if you strike down and call upon the yeomanry of Massachusetts, you find a man like this to stand forward, when the State needs him. They tell us sometimes that our people are too much like the granite of our hills. So be it. Strength and endurance, offering an unchanging face to storm and sunshine alike, are the qualities of granite and the foundations also on which a race can build a great present and a mighty future. But let it not be forgotten that, if the outside of the granite cliff is somewhat stern and gray, when you pierce its heart, you find running across it the rich warm veins of color gathered there through dim ages in which contending forces moulded the earth forms we now see about us. Again, I say we have done well to meet together in memory of such a man. He has earned our praise and our gratitude, not only for what he did and for the high titles he wore so well, but for what he was. In his life he was respected, honored, loved, and trusted. At his death the State, over which he had once been set, bowed her head in grief. But across the darkness of the sorrow comes the light which such a life sheds; for we may take to our hearts the lesson it brings, — that all is well with state and country while they breed such men as this.

THREE GOVERNORS OF MASSACHUSETTS

III

ROGER WOLCOTT [1]

" Every moment dies a man,
Every moment one is born."

THERE is much sad philosophy in these simple and familiar lines from Tennyson's famous poem. The lamp of life kindles into light by one hearthstone, only to sink down in darkness by another. Every moment death, the only absolute certainty of life, descends upon one of the children of men. Every moment some home is darkened, some family bereft, some heart saddened, perhaps broken. In some corner, no matter how small or humble, at every instant the light has gone out, and the little world of the inmates has crumbled away about them. Surely it seems to them at that dark hour that the very universe itself must have stopped too. Then comes swiftly the first harsh awakening. The stricken soul, when night has passed, looks forth,

---

[1] An address delivered at Symphony Hall in Boston on the occasion of the services in memory of Roger Wolcott, Governor of Massachusetts, 1898–1901, on April 18, 1901.

and lo! the great world of nature is unchanged.
The rising sun shoots its red shafts across the dark
waters, or gilds the city roof or country tree top
even as it did before. The twitter of birds is in
the air, the myriad sounds of life rise murmuring
from the earth, a new day is given to man, and
nature, smiling or frowning, is still the same, ever
beautiful and ever indifferent to human joy or human sorrow.

Then comes a yet sharper pang. Nature's world
moves on, and so, alas, does the world of man.
Horatio, kneeling by the body of Hamlet, lifts his
head and cries, " Why does the drum come hither? "
The prince he loved, the noble Laertes, the king and
queen, all the majesty of Denmark, lie dead about
him, slain in an instant by steel or poison. His
world is in ruins at his feet. Here assuredly is the
end of all things. And then, even then, at that
supreme moment, the sounds of life and war quiver
in the air. " Why does the drum come hither? "
All is not over, then. Another sunrise is at hand,
another day beginning. Hamlet is dead, and yet the
world is marching on just as of yore. Its drum-
beats break the tragic silence, and the coming footsteps of the new king sound in the mourner's ear.
In all the range of the greatest genius among men
there is no finer, deeper touch than in that sudden
cry from Horatio. Those few words are fraught

with more meaning than many a solemn Greek
chorus; they pierce our hearts with the eternal cry
of humanity in the first agony of sorrow; they tell
as mercilessly as the Norns of the dim Northland
that the world of nature and of men is ever moving
on its appointed way.

When, therefore, it happens that a man's death
gives pause to the march of life, when the footfall
of the columns grows faint and ceases, when the
drums are hushed and a stillness gathers over the
world in which he has played his part, then we may
know that he who has gone was one deserving of
remembrance, for his going has stayed the great
procession in its course, and there must have been
that about him which had sunk very deep into the
hearts and minds of his fellow-men. Such was the
man in whose memory we meet to-day. When he
died there came a hush over the old Commonwealth.
Among the distant hills, in crowded city streets, and
by the sounding sea men and women paused. Grief
was in their hearts, and words of sorrow on their
lips. The drums were muffled, the columns halted,
the march of life was stayed. When he was buried
the people of city and of State poured forth to do
him honor. They turned from their business or
their pleasure and bowed themselves in the house of
mourning. It was no formal sorrow, no official
grief, which thus found expression. It came from

the heart, — from the heart of a great people, who had known and loved him.

We would fain leave something behind us to tell those who come after us why we so sorrowed, and what manner of man he was for whom we grieved. We have the human yearning to bear our testimony, the testimony of those who knew him, in such fashion that the erasing finger of the fleeting years may spare it to be read by the generations yet unborn. For this purpose we have gathered here to-day. For this purpose I have been chosen to put into imperfect words that which we all feel, to express in formal and in public manner the sorrow and admiration of State and city for the man so long the first citizen and the chief magistrate of the Commonwealth.

You will pardon me if for a moment I speak with a personal accent. To be summoned to tell the life story and life work of a dear friend and contemporary is the saddest of all the labors of love. I turn to the record to draw from it the story I would repeat to you, and which we all know so well. Everything is there ready to my hand, but memory and her attendant ghosts come between me and the printed page, and will not be swept aside. I cannot see the facts and dates now. I can see only two handsome brothers, boys at school, liked by all, especially popular with the smaller boys, of whom I

am one, because they are always kind and good-
natured. Fine, manly, vigorous boys they are;
active in every sport and full of the joy of existence.
It is war time, and the school is very patriotic and
feverishly interested in soldiers and in battles.
Presently the elder of the brothers disappears from
school, and we hear that he has gone to the war.
We all think it very splendid, and wish that we too
could go and follow him.

Memories of boyhood are like dreams. They take
no heed of time. There is in memory no space
between the elder brother at school and the next
scene. In reality there was an interval of brave,
active service, even while we boys at home played on
as before. All this vanishes in recollection. He
had gone to the front, he had come home wasted
with fever, he was dead, that was all we knew.
Now the page of memory grows luminous indeed.
The school goes to his funeral, and there, in the
familiar house in Boylston Street, we see him in his
coffin, very pale and worn, dressed in the uniform of
the United States, while the younger brother stands
beside the dead, learning a lesson which is to affect
his whole life. Now we know once for all what
patriotism means. The whole scene shines out in
memory like the landscape under the flash of lightning on a summer's night.

Then the veil drops again, the years go by, and I

see the survivor of the two brothers entering college
in the same year as myself, he as sophomore and I
as freshman. Although a class ahead of me, he is
one of the well-remembered figures of my Harvard
days; handsome, kindly always, one of those who
in any place or company could never be overlooked,
and we meet constantly in societies and in the daily
life of the college. Then he passed from Cambridge.
I followed him, and we went our several ways into
the world. Presently I heard of him in city politics,
then in the legislature; then our paths again con-
verged, and he rose to be the head of the State and
of the party. Thus we came together once more, as
in the old school days, engaged now in a common
cause, and speaking many times from the same plat-
form. However often we met in this way, the pride
and pleasure I felt in watching him and in listening
to his ripening eloquence grew with each occasion,
and the pride and pleasure were of that peculiar
kind which springs up only when two men have
been boys together and friends for a lifetime.
Every time I saw him rise and address an audience
I felt a fresh glow of delight as I looked at him, and
thought how completely the stately figure, the clear
and dignified speech, the honesty of purpose and high-
minded devotion to duty which could be read in his
face and heard in his words befitted the great office
which he held. Again and again I have longed to

cry out to the world, "Look well upon him ; that
is the man whom Massachusetts chooses to represent
her ; do you wonder that we are proud of the State
which breeds such men, and gives such a successor to
Winthrop and to Andrew?" I cannot longer trust
myself with memories. They are bringing me too
near the shadowed present. They can only end in
unavailing tears. Each in our degree, we all share
in them and treasure them.

> " There 's rosemary, that 's for remembrance :
>   Pray, love, remember."

We who have known him, we shall not forget.
Let me lay down the rosemary, it is nearest to our
hearts, and from the records of the past gather up
the laurel.

No element of the English-speaking people has had
a more profound influence upon their history and fortunes, both in the old world and the new, than the
Puritans of the seventeenth century and their descendants.   From the stock of Puritan Englishmen,
pure and unmixed, Roger Wolcott derived his ancestry.   The founder of the family in New England
was Henry Wolcott, a Somersetshire gentleman, the
owner of Goldon Manor, and other estates near Tol-
land in that county.   He did not leave England
when past middle life to seek new fortunes in a new
world, but he abandoned fortune, high position, and
a generous estate in obedience to his religious beliefs,

and fared forth across the Atlantic to find a home for them in the forests of America. He reached Boston the 30th of May, 1630, settled at Dorchester, as it was named soon afterward, and moved thence, with Mr. Wareham's church, to Windsor, Connecticut. In 1637 he was chosen a member of the lower house of the legislature, and next year a member of the upper house of magistrates, to which he was annually re-elected during the remainder of his life.

Simon Wolcott, the son of the immigrant, married Martha Pitkin, the sister of the governor of the colony, and of this marriage was born Roger, in 1679. Before he was thirty Roger had become selectman of his town, and thus began his long and active career, which was at once military, judicial, and political. He was commissary of the American forces in the Canadian expedition of 1711, and second in command to Sir William Pepperell in the campaign of 1745, which resulted in the capture of Louisburg. As a lawyer he rose steadily, attaining the Supreme Bench in 1732. As a public man he reached the highest place, that of governor, to which he was chosen in 1750 and for four successive years. He was a strong, able man of high character and great vigor, possessing, evidently, in full measure the versatility of the Elizabethan Englishmen from whom he sprang.

Oliver, the son of Roger, followed in his father's

footsteps.   A captain in the old French war, he was a brigadier and afterward a major-general in the Revolution.   Again, like his father, he was a member of the Legislature and the Council, then a Probate Judge and Chief Justice of the Common Pleas.   When the Revolution came he was an active member of the Committee of Safety, for seven years a member of the Continental Congress, and a signer of the Declaration of Independence.   His son Oliver also saw service in the army during the Revolution, was admitted to the bar, and in 1789 was appointed Auditor of the Treasury by Washington.   Two years later he was made Comptroller, and in 1795, on the retirement of Hamilton, he became Secretary of the Treasury and a member of Washington's Cabinet.   In this position he continued during the Adams administration, retiring in 1800 and accepting a seat on the bench of the United States as a judge of the Circuit Court for the second district.   In 1815 he returned to his native town, and in 1817 was elected governor of Connecticut, an office which he held for ten years by successive annual elections.

Another son of the elder Oliver, and a brother of the Secretary of the Treasury, was Frederick Wolcott, who, after the fashion of his family, was distinguished in the public life of his own State, although he never entered the field of national politics.   He served the State in Legislature and Council and on the bench. He was a member of the Corporation of Yale College and conspicuous in philanthropy and all movements for the advancement of learning. He married Elizabeth Huntington, the granddaughter of Jabez Huntington, who was one of the leading patriots of Connecticut ; he and his five sons being all soldiers in the Revolutionary War, and all distinguished in the service. From this marriage was born Joshua Huntington Wolcott, who, coming as a boy to Boston, entered the counting-house of A. & A. Lawrence, rose to be a partner at the age of twenty-six, and during a long life was a successful merchant of high character, ability, and probity. In Boston he married Cornelia, the daughter of Samuel Frothingham, and by her had two sons, — Huntington, who died a soldier of the United States, and Roger, the late governor of this Commonwealth.

It is worth consideration, this genealogy which I have hastily sketched in bare outline. We have here one of the rare instances of a family which, starting in America with a man of fortune and good estate, always retained its position in the community. In the main line at least it never encountered the vicissitudes which attend nearly all families in the course of two hundred and fifty years. The name never dropped out of sight, but was always borne up by its representatives in the same place in society as that held by the founder. More remarkable still, in almost every generation there was at least one of the lineal male descendants of the first immigrant who rose to the very highest positions in military, political, and judicial life. The list of judges, governors, generals, Cabinet officers, and members of Congress in this pedigree is a long and striking one. From the days of the Somersetshire gentleman to those of the present generation, which has given a governor to Massachusetts and a brilliant Senator from Colorado to the United States, the Wolcotts, both as soldiers and civilians, have rendered service to their country, as eminent as it has been unbroken. War and statecraft were in the blood of this race, and can we wonder that they have found fitting exemplars in our own time? It is not a name made illustrious by some single ancestor in a dim past and suffered to rust unused by descendants who were content with the possession of a trade-mark. Here is a long roll of honor, where the son felt that he would be unworthy of his father if he did not add fresh lustre to the name he bore by service to his State and country, either in the hour of trial or in the pleasant paths of peace.

This, then, was the heritage, these the traditions to which Roger Wolcott fell heir when he was born in Boston on July 13, 1847. There and in Milton his boyhood was passed. He was educated at the private Latin school of Mr. E. S. Dixwell, and for a short time in Europe, whither he went with his family after his brother's death. He returned in 1867 and entered the sophomore class at Harvard in that year. He took a conspicuous place in college, and stood high, not only in his studies, but in the estimation of the faculty and in the regard of his own class and of all the students of that period. He was chosen the orator of his class, and delivered the oration on his class day in 1870. Class day orations do not, as a rule, add much to permanent literature or to the sum of human information. They generally pass away with the sunshine and the music, the cheers and the flowers of the merry day which brings them forth. But I have been struck, on reading over Governor Wolcott's class oration, with the good sense and unusual maturity of thought which it displays. These occasions are ordinarily irresistible in their temptation to a profuse use of language and to the exhibition of a wisdom or a cynicism of which happy youth is alone capable. Here in Governor Wolcott's oration there is nothing of all this. The style is sober and unstrained, and there is a central thought which is followed steadily. His plea was for the preservation of enthusiasm and faith, a gospel always worth preaching to a graduating class, disposed to be world-weary, and too seldom expounded by a student to his fellows. One sentence is so characteristic and foretells so strongly the future career

13

of the speaker that I will quote it. "No educated
man," he says, "is justified in shrinking from the
responsibility which is thrust upon him, nor is it
possible for an American citizen to wash his hands
of his country. There is no such thing as neutrality
in citizenship. He who is not with his country is
against her." Sound doctrine, strongly put; more
needed just then, I think, than now, but carrying a
truth which cannot too often be pressed home upon
the educated men of the United States.

After graduation Governor Wolcott was for two
years a tutor in French at Harvard. At the same
time he studied law, taking his degree at the Law
School in 1874, and soon after was admitted to the
Suffolk bar, although he never engaged in active
practice. Almost immediately upon leaving college
he began to take part in politics, and his beginning
was of exactly the right sort. He did not manifest
his interest in public affairs by merely criticising
those who were engaged in them, and by doleful
wailings that things generally were not better. On
the contrary, he plunged in himself and tried to
make things better by his own exertions. He took
his share of party work, went to ward meetings,
helped to get the vote registered and to bring it out,
and then distributed ballots at the polls on election
day. In 1876 he was elected to the Common Council,
where he served for three years (1877, 1878, 1879),

becoming the acknowledged leader, and being supported by his party for the presidency of that body. In 1881 he was elected to the House of Representatives in the legislature. His second year was that of General Butler as governor, — a somewhat trying period, especially to Mr. Wolcott, who was the recognized leader of the Republicans on the floor. He served three years in the legislature, winning the confidence of every one, and extending his reputation throughout the State as a man of ability, judgment, high character, and devotion to the public interests.

It was at this time, and owing to his success in the legislature, that his name was first suggested as a candidate for governor. The suggestion, without doubt, would soon have borne fruit had it not been for the course of national politics. The nomination of Mr. Blaine for the presidency was opposed by Mr. Wolcott, and when made was strongly disapproved by him. He was too earnest a Republican and too deeply attached to Republican principles to throw himself into opposition or seek to destroy his party because it had made a nomination which was distasteful to him. He contented himself by withdrawing for the time from the active political work in which he had always been so much engaged. This retirement, however, implied neither inactivity nor leisure. He had many occupations and pursuits other than politics to which he was able to devote himself, and where he could render valuable service to the public.

I have been astonished, in looking over the list of positions which he held, at the number and variety of his interests and at the work which I know these positions must have involved, especially for a man with his keen sense of responsibility. If I mention some of them, the mere recital of the names will bring a more vivid idea of the fulness of his life than any words of description could possibly do. He was a trustee of the New England Trust Company, a director of the Providence Railroad and of several manufacturing corporations. The offer once made to him of the treasurership of one of the New England mills is proof of the capacity he showed in these business positions and of the attention he gave to their duties. He was a member of the Massachusetts Historical Society and of the Society of the Cincinnati and the Society of Colonial Wars, which all appealed strongly to his love of American history, in which his ancestors had played such honorable parts. He was an overseer of Harvard, and visitor of the departments of the university. He was a vestryman of King's Chapel, a member of the Civil Service Reform and Social Science Associations, a trustee of the Massachusetts General Hospital, the Eye and Ear Infirmary, the

Boston Dispensary, and at one time a visitor among the poor for the Provident Association.

This catalogue, dry as it sounds, has deep significance. Think for a moment how business has been promoted, how literature and historical research have been advanced, how better manners and purer laws have been encouraged, and, most important of all, how much charity has been dispensed and how greatly human suffering has been relieved by the societies and corporations the names of which I have just repeated. These libraries and charities and hospitals are the glory of this community, and they must be directed by men who will work hard and take heavy responsibility without any hope or desire of personal reward. I have heard it often said that to people who have no occupation, much wealth, and some education, the United States offers nothing. I gratefully and profoundly believe in the truth of this proposition. The day is, I trust, far distant when America will furnish conditions thoroughly agreeable to idlers and triflers. But when it is said, as it sometimes is, that there is no opportunity here for men of leisure, nothing can be more false. In no country in the world is there larger and finer opportunity for the man who is master of his time, for nowhere is there more need of men who can, without pay, serve the community in the beneficent work of philanthropy, in the promotion of art and learning, and in all that makes for the relief of suffering and the uplifting of the intellectual and moral interests of our nation. Roger Wolcott was one of the men who understood this need, who regarded his own freedom from the necessity of work as a trust to be fulfilled, not as a luxury to be enjoyed, and who gave his time and strength to the service of his country and his fellow-men just as amply as a private citizen as when he held high office. It is a noble record of public service unselfishly and quietly performed, an example to be studied and followed by all those to whom fortune has been bountiful in her gifts.

Mr. Wolcott's withdrawal from politics, temporary at first, was continued on account of the illness of his father. From the time of his brother's death he had devoted himself in every way to the effort to fill a double place and make up to his parents for the loss of the elder son. Only those nearest him can appreciate fully the extent of this unselfish devotion or of the personal sacrifices he made so cheerfully, especially during his father's declining years. Like many other duties, it was fulfilled by him simply, lovingly, generously.

When comparative freedom from these absorbing cares again was his, he once more entered politics and came forward in the hour of defeat to help his party by accepting the presidency of the Republican

Club of Massachusetts, to which his leadership gave a strong impetus. This was in 1891, and in the following year (1892) he was nominated by the Republican convention as their candidate for lieutenant-governor and was elected. The defeat of the Republican candidate for governor made Mr. Wolcott, although holding only the second place in the government, the official head of the party at the State House. The position was a delicate and difficult one, for the powers of the lieutenant-governor are constitutionally very limited, and yet much was expected of him under the existing conditions. Mr. Wolcott's judgment and capacity for leadership were put to an immediate test by the question which was raised as to the ultimate power of the Council in regard to its own committees. The governor undertook to make it appear that the claim of the Council was a mere political device intended to hamper the executive for partisan reasons. This view was specious and well calculated to draw an unthinking support, but Mr. Wolcott was not to be deterred by a cry of partisanship from deciding the question on its merits. He sustained the view of the Council, and took the broad ground that the appointment of committees must always rest ultimately in the body from which they are to be chosen. His brief statement of the case, which he put upon the record, was at once clear and unanswerable. The attempt to

make his action obnoxious as the result of unscru-
pulous partisanship fell to the ground, for no man
was more free from such tendencies than he. Mr.
Wolcott was never extreme, and political bitterness
was impossible to him. By nature he was broad
and tolerant, and he was too independent and too
exacting in his ideals ever to be an unreasoning
partisan. Yet no man was ever more deeply wedded
to the great beliefs and fundamental principles of
the party in which he had been born and bred, and
which he supported steadily and strongly throughout his life. He valued and cherished personal independence, but he did not confound independence
with bitter and chaotic opposition to everything
which exists, and he understood history too well not
to be aware that representative government has been
more or less a failure in every country where the
system of two great and responsible parties, one of
government and one of opposition, has not prevailed
as it always has prevailed among the English-speaking
people.

In his speech to the Republican Club on April 8,
1891, Mr. Wolcott defined his position on the question of political parties and personal independence,
and in these vigorous sentences he laid down the
principle by which he himself was guided. He said
on that occasion : " No word of mine shall ever be
uttered to depreciate that robust and virile inde-

pendence in politics which holds country and honor above party, which, while acting within party lines, ever strives to secure the best in men and measures, and, often buffeted and defeated, never ceases to wage war upon dishonesty and chicanery, using party as a weapon, but never wearing it as a yoke. But the independent, who prides himself upon being a total abstainer, until the day of election, from all lot or part in political movements, should be treated as those who skulk when the bugle sounds."

In 1893 Mr. Wolcott was renominated for lieutenant governor, with Mr. Greenhalge as the candidate for governor. Both were elected, and the same ticket was renominated and re-elected in 1894 and 1895 by large and increasing majorities. On March 5, 1896, Governor Greenhalge, honored and beloved, died in office, and Mr. Wolcott became the acting governor of the Commonwealth. He assumed the office of the chief executive under sad circumstances, which no one felt more deeply than he, for he was sincerely attached to his associate and predecessor. But he came to his new place possessed of an unusual familiarity with all its duties, drawn from nearly four years of experience as lieutenant-governor. The affairs of the State moved on smoothly and easily under his guidance, without any sign of disturbance.

In the autumn of 1896 Mr. Wolcott was unani-

mously nominated by the Republican convention as
their candidate for governor. No one else indeed
was mentioned, or even thought of. Not merely had
he borne himself so well as acting governor that it
would have been impossible to have displaced him,
but in his years of service as lieutenant-governor he
had established himself firmly in the good opinion of
the people, and had gained a strong hold upon their
affection. In these years they had come to know
him. He had appeared much in public, and had
made speeches on many subjects, by no means confined to the political questions of the day. Always
dignified, thoughtful, and interesting, he grew and
developed with constant practice until he became
one of the best speakers in the State. Gifted with a
commanding presence and a powerful, ringing voice,
he at once held the attention of his audiences. He
had an ample vocabulary and a cultivated style and
diction. On the many occasions and celebrations at
which our governors are expected to appear he not
only always said something worth hearing, something serious and weighty, showing alike good sense
and careful thought, but he was graceful and felici-
tous, and had a capacity for happy humor with which
he was largely and fortunately endowed. In dis-
cussing the great questions of the day relating to the
tariff and the currency he showed himself master of
his subject, and his arguments were cogent and well

knit, effective and convincing. He put his points sharply and strongly, often with a glow of eloquence, and sometimes with epigrammatic force, as when at the ratification meeting of 1896 he spoke of the " honor Democrats," a phrase which went all over the country. When he became acting governor he had already demonstrated to the State not only his character and his fitness for public affairs, but he had proved that he was an eloquent speaker, and able to deal as a statesman with the largest public questions. Thus the nomination for the first place went to him by general accord, and with the most widespread and genuine enthusiasm. He took a leading part in the great national campaign of that year in Massachusetts, and was elected by a phenomenal majority, the largest ever given to a governor.

Mr. Wolcott held the governorship for three years, being re-elected by majorities surpassed only by that which he himself received in 1896. Owing to the growth of population, the duties of the chief executive of Massachusetts have greatly increased of late years, and now entail a heavy burden of work upon any man with a strong sense of responsibility. This feeling of responsibility was especially keen in Governor Wolcott. Every interest of the State was the subject of his personal and thoughtful care. Prisons, asylums, and reformatories, the care of the poor, the criminal and the insane, schools, railroads, gas and insurance, harbors and lands, municipal government, parks, water, roads, and the enforcement of law, — all these matters and many others demanded knowledge, study, and care, and all received them from him in full measure. He never shirked or neglected anything. Many difficult and debated questions of legislation also arose, and every law sent to him received his thorough consideration. He never sought to shift responsibility upon the legislature, but took always his entire share as part of the lawmaking power. More than once he felt obliged to differ from the legislature, and he was always ready when it seemed to him his duty to use the veto. These questions are still too near to be discussed on their merits here, even if time permitted and it were appropriate to do so. But I think no one can read over those veto messages and not be struck by their clearness and force and impressed by their sound reasoning. Governor Wolcott was not only wisely cautious, but he was almost morbidly anxious to be exactly just in dealing with any disputed question. He would weigh and consider all arguments, and look at both sides, but when he had reached his conclusion, when he had made up his mind as to where his duty lay, he was entirely fearless, and signed or vetoed, as the case might be, without any regard for consequences. In his messages and State papers it is easy to discern the consistent policy which runs through them all. He looked for guidance to the interests of the State and to the broad political principles in which he believed. When he had once made up his mind in what direction these public interests lay, he was not to be turned aside either by the pressure of great corporations, or by clamor from without, or by anxiety as to the effect of his action upon his own fortunes. Righteousness and the welfare of the Commonwealth in all questions, whether personal or political, were, when doubt and conflict arose, his ultimate guides, the oracles from whose decisions there was no appeal.

The administration of the ordinary business of the State is enough to test any man's strength or make any man's reputation, but to Mr. Wolcott there came a burden and a trial which are not imposed more than once in a generation upon the governor of a State. His term of office came at the moment when the nation entered upon a new epoch in its history. In 1898 war was declared with Spain, and the President called for troops. The manner in which Massachusetts responded was in keeping with her past, and added a new glory to her history. As in the Revolution and the Civil War, she offered the national government more than her quota, and place could not be found for all the regiments and batteries which sought service. The thorough equipment of the Massachusetts troops, and the rapidity with which they went forward in complete readiness for service gratified and surprised the government at Washington. All this is history and known of all men, but that which is not so well understood is the extent to which the condition of the regiments and the rapidity of their mobilization were due to the watchful care and unresting energy of the governor. We had an excellent militia and a fine and well-trained staff, but in military matters more depends upon the chief than in any other department. Governor Wolcott supervised everything, and his spirit informed all those who obeyed his orders. He sent in a message asking for an emergency fund of half a million dollars, and in twenty-five minutes the bill had passed both Houses and the money was in his hands, a mark of confidence in him as fine as the unhesitating patriotism of the legislature in the presence of war.

But the governor's duties did not stop there. It was for him to spend the money and carry on the work. He went to every camp and quickened every movement, he thought and labored for the equipment, and it was his voice which bade the soldiers God-speed, and in lofty and inspiring words sent them forth to fight for their country with the blessing of Massachusetts upon them. He kept the same watch over the soldiers in the field, and when they returned from the war, many of them wasted with fever, he was the first to meet them on the transport or the railroad train, the first to greet them and to say to them, " Well done," in the name of the Commonwealth. He went among them, stood by their cots, gentle and sympathetic as a woman, strong and encouraging as a man. With his own hands he ministered to them, and from his own purse he often fed them ; he aided them in every way, he was much more than their commander, he was their friend. In all his career of distinguished public service I like best to think of Roger Wolcott as he appeared at that moment; and the recollection of that gracious, stately figure among the sick, the wounded, and the dying, bringing hope and comfort with the authority of high place and the tenderness of love, will ever be one of the cherished and beautiful memories of Massachusetts.

In January, 1900, Mr. Wolcott retired from the governorship. For seven years he had been in the service of the State, and during the last four his work had been anxious and incessant. He went with his family to Europe for a much-needed, well-earned rest. He was in the prime of his powers, as vigorous physically as he was mentally, for he had always lived a wholesome life, and was a lover of outdoor air and exercise and an admirable rider. Every one looked forward to his having many years before him of distinguished service in the larger national field, and with his ripe experience winning fresh honors for himself and for the State. Opportunities indeed came quickly. President McKinley asked him to be a commissioner to the Philippines, one of the most important places in the whole range of statesmanship, but private reasons obliged him to decline. Later in the summer, when General Draper, to the regret of every one, resigned, I had the pleasure of joining with Senator Hoar in the request that Governor Wolcott might be sent to Rome. The President immediately offered him the Italian embassy, and I longed to have him take it, not because he was my friend, but because I felt so much pride in the thought of having the United States represented in Europe by such a man. Again, however, he was compelled to refuse on account of personal and family reasons. He returned to Boston in time to make one speech for his party and to cast his vote for President McKinley. It was a joy to have him again among us, looking so well and with so much promise for a brilliant future.

> "The hope of unaccomplished years
> Seemed large and lucid round his brow."

But it was not to be. The hand of death was on him even then. Before the year closed he was gone, and the whole State was mourning by his grave.

To tell the story of a life filled with action and

achievement within the limits of an address such as this is impossible. No one knows how inadequate, how barren the meagre outline is, so well as he who attempts it. Yet it is still possible to learn something, even from the dry facts so hurriedly rehearsed. Here was a man born to all that men most desire. He was strong, handsome, vigorous in mind and body. He had wealth and position. He was fortunate in his birth, fortunate in his ancestry, thrice fortunate in his marriage and in his home. Here was strong temptation to ease, to repose, to self-indulgence, or to an existence of cultured leisure. They were all put aside for an active, earnest life, filled with hard work. At the very beginning it seems as if he had taken as his rule the injunction which Dante puts into the mouth of Ulysses :

> " Considerate la vostra semenza,
>   Fatti non foste a viver come bruti,
>   Ma per seguir virtude e conoscenza."

When all is done it looks simple enough, but only a man of strong will and determined purpose can do it. Some one may say that ambition was the cause. Every man who comes to anything has the righteous ambition to do something in the world and to do it well, but that is a quality, not a cause, and too often ends in ineffectual longing. Ambition is but a shallow explanation. Remember that the seven

years of high place and large powers were preceded
by more than twenty years of hard work for the
public service, both in private and political life;
work without personal gain, and which might never
bring any outward reward. The truth lies deeper
than this. Roger Wolcott felt instinctively that
every man owes a debt to his country, and that the
greater the gifts of fortune the larger the debt, the
heavier the responsibility. That debt he meant to
pay, that responsibility he meant to meet, and so he
turned from ease and pleasure to hard work for
public ends. This is a noble and just conception of
a man's duty, nowhere so necessary as in this Republic, and it was his in full measure. To those
placed as he was at the opening of life I would say,
Look well upon him and strive to imitate him, remembering that great as were the honors he won,
that which was better than place or title was the
high ideal of duty as a man and as a citizen, which
led him to put aside all temptations to ease and
quiet and go down into the arena of life to fight a
good fight in the great world of men.

He was well equipped for the struggle. He had
health and strength, natural ability, a liberal education, a vigorous, well-trained mind, always alert and
open, great capacity for work, and an industry which
never failed. One essential condition of success in
such a career as Mr. Wolcott's is the capacity to deal

with other men, and this quality was his in abundance. He was simple and democratic in his ways,
with the manners of a thorough man of the world,
always attractive, easy, and without pretence, and
yet never undignified or weakly familiar. Here, too,
his strong sense of humor and love of fun were of
inestimable service to him as they are to all men, for
those who possess them are saved from that most
fatal of errors, taking one's self too seriously and
mistaking one's relation to the universe. He was
entirely free from the small vanities and jealousies
and the morbid absorption in self which are the
bane of so many excellent persons in all walks of
public life, and which do more to alienate friends and
give lasting offence than much more serious faults.
All these qualities commended him to his fellow-men,
but that which won most was his clear common-
sense and honesty of judgment, quickly felt by all
who were engaged with him in serious affairs, either
of public or private business.

More valuable still was the fact that he kept
always an open mind. He was ready to learn and
did learn as he advanced, and was always growing
and developing. His opinions never hardened into
prejudices, new questions and policies did not frighten
him, and as he grew older, instead of stiffening, he
became more kindly and more tolerant. Nothing illustrates this better than his feeling about his country

and his people. Intensely patriotic by nature, stimulated in patriotism by his bringing up and by his
brother's death, his feeling about his country and a
man's duty to it shines forth in the words which I
have quoted from his class oration. Then he had
thirty years of experience in the rough, eager, com-
bative world of this young and mighty democracy.
It made him neither hard nor cynical, nor a slave to
that dangerous wisdom which sneers and doubts.
This wide experience among men wrought with him,
as I think it must always work with every open, just,
and generous mind, and near the close of his life he
said in a speech : "If I have learned nothing else
since I have held office, I have learned to believe in
the American people. I have learned to believe that
virtue is more common than vice, that noble manhood and womanhood have not died out among us.
I believe God has made the law of progress, not a
law of retrogression, and I urge you young men not
to give way to pessimism. Be courageous, be hope-
ful. Believe in the destiny of America, believe in
the purpose of Almighty God, believe with all hope
in the future." This is not the shallow optimism of
respectable " gigmanity " which thinks everything is
for the best in the best of all possible worlds, and
upon which Voltaire turned his fatal smile. It is
the faith of a man who knows well that there is
much wrong, much suffering, much sin in the world,

who has striven to make his corner of it better and brighter, and who has come through the trial with a larger hope, and a profounder belief in the American people and in their capacity for great tasks, with a deeper love for his country, and an assured confidence in the future of his race.

This faith in his people and his country made the people trust Governor Wolcott, for they refuse their confidence to those who distrust them. But there were other and deeper reasons for their faith in him and for the love they bore him, which has been so strikingly manifested since his death. They recognized his ability, his eloquence, his industry, his conscientiousness, his entire fitness for high place, his fearlessness when duty spoke to him. Yet it was something other than these great qualities which appealed to them most of all. He was a good man. I know the ready sneer which too often greets these words in this world of ours. If hypocrisy is the homage which vice pays to virtue, it is equally true that there is the hypocrisy of evil which is the tribute timid virtue pays to vice. Hence the ready sneer. Yet when one of the greatest geniuses of the last century and one of the bravest of men lay dying, the best he could find to say to a man he loved as his son was, " Be a good man, my dear." Was there ever a more tender or a better message from any human death-ded ? I think not, and I know well that the goodness which Walter Scott intended, and which we all reverence in our hearts even if we close our lips, was not that narrow self-righteousness which is as worthless as the tinkling cymbal, but the goodness which includes among its chief virtues a large and gentle charity toward others.

Such was the goodness of Governor Wolcott. The bright mirror of his life was never dimmed by the faintest breath of reproach. What he seemed, that he was, and the people knew it. They knew, too, that he had courage; I do not mean physical courage or moral courage, both of which were his, but just the plain courage which resists temptation by instinct, as a man defends his mother or his wife. He might make mistakes; all successful men, doers of deeds, are sure to make them. "To err is human." But whatever chanced, the people of Massachusetts knew that there were certain things of which Roger Wolcott was utterly incapable. Whatever he did or did not do, they knew that no mean, base motive, no personal or illicit gain, no degrading hope, could ever move him or ever be possible to him. " Whatever record leaped to light, he never could be shamed." The people knew all this, knew it by their wise instinct, and so they loved and trusted Governor Wolcott with a rare confidence and affection.

They were proud of him, too, as they had good

reason to be. They liked to look upon such a governor, and they liked to think that the State on great occasions was represented beyond its own borders and in the eyes of the world by such a man. The feeling of the people of Massachusetts in regard to their governors is a strong and peculiar one. The State has a respect and an admiration for its chief magistrate which exist in no such degree elsewhere. The sentiment is an honor to State and people. It is traditional and deep rooted. It is also well founded. We have had governors in this Commonwealth now for nearly three centuries. The list is a long one, but I do not believe that anywhere in the world is to be found a line of chief magistrates of equal length where you can discover so little that is unworthy, so little that is commonplace, so much that is eminent and honorable and of good report. The standard is a high one. The succession is a just pride to the State. To lower that standard would be grievous. To maintain it is much for any man to do. To lift it still higher is given to few. Yet this, I think, Roger Wolcott did. He added new lustre to that shining roll, and earned the right to be named among the chosen few where Andrew and Winthrop stand together. All this, again, the people knew well. Need we wonder that they loved Governor Wolcott, and that as they loved him so also they were proud of him? The love and pride of the people whom he served, the devotion of the loyal friends so loved by him, an unblemished record, a life filled with good work done and with honorable achievements which have passed now into the history of State and country, here are titles and distinctions with which those who most honor his memory may well be content.

Yet the greatest is behind, for we can say with truth of Roger Wolcott that he is most highly to be praised and most fondly to be remembered for what he was rather than for what he did. Greater honor hath no man than this, to be loved and honored and held in memory, not so much for the deeds he did, or the great places he filled, or even for the work he wrought, as for what he himself was as a man.   There is a type of man which we of the English-speaking people hold in especial honor, and like to think, justly, as I believe, peculiar to our race and history.   It is a type which knows neither class nor rank.   The man may be rich or poor, humble or great, the champion of village rights or the defender of a nation's liberties. But all such men have certain traits in common : simplicity of character, willingness to bear the burdens of the community, to do their public duty wherever it may lead, and always without personal ambition or thought of self.   It may be John Brown, the poor Scotch carrier, shot down by Claverhouse as he lifts his hands in prayer, or that other John Brown, walking to the gallows in Virginia, or Sydney on the scaffold, or Robert Shaw falling upon the slopes of Wagner. They may come to martyrdom or death in battle, or they may never go beyond the peaceful service of their native town, or the higher service of poor and suffering humanity. Their light may shine before men, or do no more than warm and brighten some little corner. Commanding ability or high genius may be given or denied to them, but great character must always be theirs and perfect readiness to serve their fellow-men, whether in the sheltered times of peace or in the hour of fierce trial, when the last sacrifice may be demanded.

The great exemplars in history of the type I mean, and of which description is so difficult, are Hampden and Washington, the one a country gentleman of moderate talent and slight achievement, the other one of the greatest leaders, soldiers, and statesmen of all time; but both alike in their ready self-sacrifice to the public weal, in their ideals of conduct, in their performance of duty without hope or desire of place or power, shine out upon the pages of history. It is one of the glories of our race that such men have never been lacking in our history, and in this noble company I think Roger Wolcott stands. May we not rejoice that in the nineteenth century New England could breed such a man, and must we not rejoice still more that a man of this fine type and nature commanded the affection, the trust, and the pride of this proud old State? Profound gratitude for a life and character like this mingles with our sorrow as we stand by his untimely grave.

> " Lofty designs must close in like effects;
>   Loftily lying,
>   Leave him — still loftier than the world suspects,
>   Living and dying."

THE TREATY-MAKING POWERS OF THE SENATE

THE action of the Senate upon the first Hay-Pauncefote treaty in December, 1900, gave rise to much discussion not only in regard to the merits of the treaty and of the Senate amendments, but also as to the rights and functions of the Senate as part of the treaty-making power. That there should be differences of opinion as to the merits of the questions involved in the treaty is entirely natural, but it seems strange that there should be any misapprehension as to the functions and powers of the Senate, because those are not matters of opinion but well-established facts, simple in themselves and clearly defined both by law and precedent. Yet such misapprehension not only existed but was manifested here and there in the United States by statements and arguments as confident as they were erroneous. The English newspapers, as a rule, of course did not know anything about the powers of the Senate, but seemed to have a general belief that the Senate amendments were in some way a gross breach of faith, a view not susceptible of explanation, but very soothing to those who held it, and quite characteristic. It is, however, a much more serious matter when misapprehension of this kind is found among those who are charged with the conduct of government. It is their duty and their business to understand thoroughly the institutions, constitutional provisions, and political methods of other countries with which they are obliged to have dealings and to maintain relations. We have a right to expect that Lord Lansdowne, a statesman of long experience, who has held some of the highest offices under the British Crown, who has been advanced from the great post of Secretary of War to the still greater one of Secretary of State for Foreign Affairs, should understand thoroughly the constitutional provisions and modes of governmental procedure in the United States. Yet we find in Lord Lansdowne's note to Lord Pauncefote of February 22, 1901, in reference to the Senate amendments the following statement :

" The Clayton-Bulwer treaty is an international contract of unquestioned validity ; a contract which, according to well-established international usage, ought not to be abrogated or modified save with the consent of both the parties to the contract. His Majesty's Government find themselves confronted with a proposal communicated to them by the United States Government, without any previous attempt to ascertain their views, for the abrogation of the Clayton-Bulwer treaty."

The meaning of this passage, taken as a whole, is not very clear, and in the last clause it contains at least one singular proposition. Admitting the international usage to be as Lord Lansdowne states it, the Hay-Pauncefote negotiation conformed to it strictly. The sole purpose of the Hay-Pauncefote treaty was to modify, by amicable agreement, the Clayton-Bulwer treaty. So far as the Hay-Pauncefote treaty went, it modified the Clayton-Bulwer treaty, and to that extent superseded it. How far it superseded it was a disputed point. It was strongly argued here that the Hay-Pauncefote treaty *ex necessitate* superseded entirely the Clayton-Bulwer treaty, and those Senators who advocated the insertion of the words " which is hereby superseded " were generally held to be over-cautious. It was, in fact, this division of opinion as to the extent to which the Clayton-Bulwer treaty had been superseded which led to the adoption of the first Senate amendment, but Lord Lansdowne's note shows that those who desired a specific statement of the supersession of the Clayton-Bulwer treaty were right in their construction, that the supersession was not complete as the Hay-Pauncefote treaty originally stood.[1]

[1] The second Hay-Pauncefote treaty embodied all the principles contained in the Senate amendments to the first treaty, and was ratified, December 16, 1901, by a vote of 72 to 6.

The point, however, to which I wish to draw attention here is quite different from the question of the supersession of the Clayton-Bulwer treaty in whole or in part by the first Hay-Pauncefote treaty, and is contained in the last sentence of the passage I have quoted. Lord Lansdowne there complains that his Government is confronted by a proposal from the United States without any previous attempt to ascertain their views. Here is where his misapprehension of our Constitution appears. If Mr. Hay had proposed to Lord Pauncefote, at any stage of their discussion, to insert clauses like the Senate amendments, the proposal might have been accepted or rejected, but no complaint would or could have been made that His Majesty's Government was confronted by a proposal upon which their views had not been previously ascertained. Such propositions, coming from Mr. Hay, would have been entirely germane to the purpose of the negotiation, even if they had extended to a simple, wholly unconditional abrogation of the Clayton-Bulwer treaty, and would have been so recognized. What actually happened was that these propositions were offered at a later stage of the negotiation by the other part of the American treaty-making power in the only manner in which they could then be offered, and are therefore no more a subject of just complaint on account of the manner of their presentation than if they had been put forward at an earlier stage by Mr. Hay.   If we follow the negotiation through its different phases, what has just been stated becomes apparent.   Mr. Hay and Lord Pauncefote open a negotiation for the modification of the Clayton-Bulwer treaty in such manner as to remove the obstacles which it may present to the construction of the Central American canal by the United States.   After due discussion they agree upon and sign a treaty.   That agreement, so far as Great Britain is concerned, requires only the approval of the King for its completion, but with the United States the case is very different, because no treaty can be ratified by the President of the United States without the consent of the Senate.   The treaty, so called, is therefore still inchoate, a mere project for a treaty, until the consent of the Senate has been given to it.   That all treaties must be submitted to the Senate, and obtain the Senate's approval before they can be ratified and become binding upon the United States, was, we may assume, well known to Lord Lansdowne.   But he does not seem to have realized that the Senate could properly continue the negotiation begun by Mr. Hay and Lord Pauncefote by offering new or modified propositions to His Majesty's Government.   Of this he was clearly not informed, or he would not have made the complaint about being confronted with new propositions, as if something unusual and unfair had been done. No one expects the "man in the street" or the London editor to remember that so long ago as 1795 the Senate made an entirely new amendment to the Jay treaty and that England accepted it, or that so recently as March, 1900, the Senate made amendments to the treaty regulating the tenure and disposition of the property of aliens and that England accepted them, or that it has been the uniform practice of the Senate to amend treaties, whenever it seemed their duty to do so. But a British secretary of state for foreign affairs is, of course, familiar with all these things and ought, therefore, to realize that the Senate can only present its views to a foreign government by formulating them in the shape of amendments, which the foreign government may reject, or accept, or meet with counter propositions, but of which it has no more right to complain than it has to complain of the offer of any germane proposition at any other stage of the negotiation.

With misapprehension like this existing not only in the British foreign office and the London Press, but also in the minds of one or two exceptionally "able" editors and correspondents in this country, who spoke of the Senate's action in amending the Hay-Pauncefote treaty as a modern usurpation, it seems not amiss to explain briefly the nature and history of the treaty-making power in the United States. The explanation is easy. It rests, indeed, on constitutional provisions so simple and on precedents so notorious that one feels inclined to begin with an apology for stating anything at once so familiar and so rudimentary. Yet it would appear that the circumstances just set forth fully justify both the explanation of the law and the statement of the facts of history.

The power to make treaties is at once a badge and an inherent right of every sovereign and independent nation. The thirteen American colonies of Great Britain, as part of the British Empire and as dependencies of the British Crown, were not sovereign nations and did not possess the treaty-making power. That power was vested in the British Crown, and when exercised the colonies were bound by the action and agreements of the British Government. When the thirteen colonies jointly and severally threw off their allegiance to the British Crown and became independent, all the usual rights of sovereignty which they had not before possessed vested, without restriction, in each one of the thirteen States. The treaty-making power was exercised accordingly by the Continental Congress, which represented all the States and where the vote was taken by States. Under the subsequent Articles of Confederation the treaty-making

15

power could not be exercised by any State alone
or by two or more States without the consent of
the United States in Congress, and was vested in
the Congress of the Confederation, where, as in the
Continental Congress, each State had one vote, and
where the assent of nine States was required to
ratify a treaty. From this it will be observed that
this sovereign right which had vested absolutely
in each State, although it was confided to the Congress of the United States, was kept wholly within
the control of the States as such, and was never
permitted to become an executive function. This
was the practice and this the precedent which the
Convention found before them when they met in
Philadelphia in 1787 to frame a new constitution,
and they showed no disposition to depart from
either. The States were very jealous of their sovereign rights, among which the power to make treaties was one of the most important, and having
so recently emerged from a colonial condition, they
were also very suspicious and very much afraid
of dangerous foreign influences, especially in the
making of treaties. At the outset, therefore, it
seems to have been the universal opinion that the
relations of the United States with other nations
should be exclusively managed and controlled by
the representatives of the States, as such, in the
Senate. The strength and prevalence of this feeling

are best shown by the various plans for a constitution presented to the Convention. The Virginian plan so called was embodied in resolutions offered by Mr. Randolph, which proposed to enlarge and amend the Articles of Confederation and passed over without mention the treaty-making power, accepting apparently the existing system which vested it in the States voting as such through their representatives. The plan offered by Mr. Pinckney provided that :

" The Senate shall have the sole and exclusive power to declare war, and to make treaties, and to appoint ambassadors and other ministers to foreign nations, and judges of the Supreme Court."

The New Jersey plan offered by Mr. Patterson, which aimed only at a mild amendment of the Articles of Confederation, left the treaty-making power, as under the Confederation, wholly within the control of the States voting as such in Congress.

Hamilton, who went to the other extreme from the New Jersey plan, gave the treaty-making power in his scheme to the President and the Senate, but conferred on the Senate alone the power to declare war.

All these plans, as well as the general resolutions agreed upon after weeks of debate, went to a committee of detail, which, on August 6, reported, through Mr. Rutledge, the first draft of the Constitution.

Section 1 of Article 9 of this first draft provided that " The Senate of the United States shall have power to make treaties and to appoint ambassadors and judges of the Supreme Court."

The manner in which this clause, as reported by the committee of detail, was modified is best described by Mr. George Ticknor Curtis in his " Constitutional History of the United States ": [1]

The power to make treaties, which had been given to the Senate by the committee of detail, and which was afterwards transferred to the President, to be exercised with the advice and consent of two-thirds of the Senators present, was thus modified on account of the changes which the plan of government had undergone, and which have been previously explained. The power to declare war having been vested in the whole legislature, it was necessary to provide the mode in which a war was to be terminated. As the President was to be the organ of communication with other governments, and as he would be the general guardian of the national interests, the negotiation of a treaty of peace, and of all other treaties, was necessarily confided to him. But as treaties would not only involve the general interests of the nation, but might touch the particular interests of individual States, and whatever their effect, were to be part of the supreme law of the land, it was necessary to give to the Senators, as the direct representatives of States, a concurrent authority with the President over the relations to be affected by them. The rule of ratification suggested by the committee to whom this subject was last confided was that

[1] Vol. i. pp. 579-581, last edition.

a treaty might be sanctioned by two-thirds of the Senators present, but not by a smaller number. A question was made, however, and much considered, whether treaties of peace ought not to be subjected to a different rule. One suggestion was that the Senate ought to have power to make treaties of peace without the concurrence of the President on account of his possible interest in the continuance of a war from which he might derive power and importance. But an objection, strenuously urged, was that if the power to make a treaty of peace were confided to the Senate alone, and a majority or two-thirds of the whole Senate were to be required to make such a treaty, the difficulty of obtaining peace would be so great that the legislature would be unwilling to make war on account of the fisheries, the navigation of the Mississippi, and other important objects of the Union. On the other hand, it was said that a majority of the States might be a minority of the people of the United States, and that the representatives of a minority of the nation ought not to have power to decide the conditions of peace.

The result of these various objections was a determination on the part of a large majority of the States not to make treaties of peace an exception to the rule, but to provide a uniform rule for the ratification of all treaties. The rule of the Confederation, which had required the assent of nine States in Congress to every treaty or alliance, had been found to work great inconvenience, as any rule must do which should give to a minority of States power to control the foreign relations of the country. The rule established by the Constitution, while it gives to every State an opportunity to be present and to vote, requires no positive quorum of the Senate for the ratification of a treaty; it simply demands that the treaty shall receive the assent of two-thirds of all the members who may be present. The theory of the Constitution undoubtedly is that the President represents the people of the United States generally and the Senators represent their respective States, so that by the concurrence which the rule thus requires the necessity for a fixed quorum of the States is avoided and the operations of this function of the Government are greatly facilitated and simplified. The adoption also of that part of the rule which provides that the Senate may either " advise or consent," enables that body so far to initiate a treaty as to propose one for the consideration of the President — although such is not the general practice.

The obvious fact that the President must be the representative of the country in all dealings with foreign nations, and that the Senate in its very nature could not, like the Chief Executive, initiate and conduct negotiations, compelled the convention to confer upon him an equal share in the power to make treaties. This was an immense concession by the States, and they had no idea of giving up their ultimate control to a president elected by the people generally. Here, therefore, is the reason for the provision of the Constitution which makes the consent of the Senate by a two-thirds majority necessary to the ratification of any treaty projected or prepared by the President. The required assent of the Senate is the reservation to the States of an equal share in the sovereign power of making treaties which before the adoption of the Constitution was theirs without limit or restriction. The treaty clause, as finally agreed to by the convention and ratified by the States, is as follows: "He [the President] shall have power, by and with the advice and consent of the Senate, to make treaties, provided two-thirds of the Senators present concur, and he shall nominate and by and with the advice and consent of the Senate shall appoint ambassadors," etc.

I have quoted the provision in regard to appointments in order to define more fully the previous one relating to treaties. The use of the words "advice and consent" in both provisions has given rise to misapprehensions in some minds, and even in one instance at least to the astounding proposition that because the Senate cannot amend a nomination by striking out the name sent in by the President and inserting another, it therefore, by analogy, cannot amend a treaty. It is for this reason well to note that the carefully phrased section gives the President absolute and unrestricted right to nominate, and the Senate can only advise and consent to the appointment of, a given person. All right to interfere in the remotest degree with the power of nomination and the consequent power of selection is wholly taken from the Senate. Very different is the wording in the treaty clause. There the words "by and with the advice and consent of"

come in after the words "shall have power" and
before the power referred to is defined. The "advice
and consent of the Senate" are therefore coextensive
with the "power" conferred on the President, which
is "to make treaties," and apply to the entire process of treaty making. The States in the convention
of 1787 agreed to share the treaty power with the
President created by the Constitution, but they
never thought of resigning it, or of retaining anything less than they gave.

The Senate, being primarily a legislative body,
cannot in the nature of things initiate a negotiation with another nation, for they have no authority
to appoint or to receive ambassadors or ministers.
But in every other respect, under the language of
the Constitution and in the intent of the framers,
they stand on a perfect equality with the President
in the making of treaties. They have an undoubted
right to recommend either that a negotiation be
entered upon or that it be not undertaken, and
I shall show presently that this right has been
exercised and recognized in both directions. As a
matter of course, the President would not be bound
by a resolution declaring against opening a negotiation, but such a resolution passed by a two-thirds
vote would probably be effective and would serve
to stop any proposed negotiation, as we shall see
was the case under President Lincoln. In the same

way the Senate has the right to advise the President
to enter upon a negotiation, and has exercised this
right more than once. Here, again, the President
is not bound to comply with the resolution, for
his power is equal and co-ordinate with that of
the Senate, but such action on the part of the
Senate, no doubt, would always have due weight.
That this right to advise or disapprove the opening
of negotiations has been very rarely exercised is
unquestionably true in practice, and the practice
is both sound and wise; but the right remains
none the less, just as the Constitution gave it, not
impaired in any way by the fact that it has been
but little used.

The right of the Senate to share in treaty making
at any stage has always been fully recognized, both
by the Senate and the Executive, not only at the
beginning of the Government, when the President
and many Senators were drawn from among the
framers of the Constitution and were, therefore,
familiar with their intentions, but at all periods
since. A brief review of some of the messages
of the Presidents and of certain resolutions of the
Senate will show better than any description the
relations between the two branches of the treaty-
making power in the United States, the uniform
interpretation of the Constitution in this respect,
and the precedents which have been established.

On August 21, 1789, President Washington noti-
fied the Senate that he would meet with them on
the following day to advise with them as to the
terms of a treaty to be negotiated with the Southern
Indians. On August 22, in accordance with this
notice, the President came into the Senate Chamber,
attended by General Knox, and laid before the
Senate a statement of facts, together with certain
questions, in regard to our relations to the Indians
of the Southern district, upon which he asked the
advice of the Senate. On August 24, 1789, he
appeared again in the Senate Chamber with General
Knox, and the discussion of our relations with the
Southern Indians was resumed. The Senate finally
voted on the questions put to it by the President,
and in that way gave him their advice.[1]

[1] During the first years of its existence the Senate sat with closed
doors, and there is no record of any of its debates. The only official
records we possess are the dry entries of the Journal, stating the
questions put and the votes. For the first two years, however, we
have an account of the doings of the Senate in the diary of William
Maclay, a Senator from Pennsylvania during the period from 1789 to
1791. In that diary (pages 129 to 133) there is a full description of
what happened upon the only occasion when a President personally
met with the Senate to consider a treaty, a mode of consideration
which was undoubtedly contemplated as the most suitable at the
time of the framing of the Constitution. In reading Mr. Maclay's
narrative it is well to remember that he was one of those persons
who are never satisfied in regard to their own integrity unless they
impugn the conduct and suspect the motives of every one else, and
especially of those who differ with them in opinion. Mr. Maclay was
exceedingly hostile to Washington and could not appreciate him.
His opinions as to men are curious and untrustworthy, but his state-

On August 11, 1790, President Washington, in a
written message, asked whether it was the judgment
of the Senate that overtures should be made to the

ments of facts, and as to what actually occurred, may as a rule
be accepted, and are of peculiar interest, because we possess no other
account of Senate debates at that period.

In the same connection there is an interesting story told in the
diary of John Quincy Adams which is worth repeating, and which
throws an interesting light upon the incident.

" Mr. Crawford told twice over the story of President Washington's
having at an early period of his Administration gone to the Senate
with a project of a treaty to be negotiated and been present at their
deliberations upon it.   They debated it and proposed alterations,
so that when Washington left the Senate Chamber he said he would
be damned if he ever went there again.   And ever since that time
treaties have been negotiated by the Executive before submitting
them to the consideration of the Senate.

" The President said he had come into the Senate about eighteen
months after the first organization of the present Government, and
then heard that something like this had occurred.

" Crawford then repeated the story, varying the words, so as to
say that Washington swore he would never go to the Senate again."
(Memoirs of John Quincy Adams, vol. vi. p. 427.)

Washington's attempt to confer with the Senate in this direct way
was so obviously inconvenient, and the discussion upon the propositions was so annoying to the President on the one side, while the
restraint of the President's presence was so much felt by the Senate
on the other, that personal deliberation between the Chief Executive
and his constitutional advisers was then and there abandoned.

But although given up in practice, the original theory that the President at his pleasure was to consult personally with the Senate upon
executive business was never laid aside.   In the first set of rules
adopted by the Senate in 1789 the idea was so much a matter of
course, apparently, that no provision is made for the forms to be
observed when the President meets with the Senate in executive session.
In the revised Rules adopted March 26, 1806, rule 34 treating of
nominations provides that : " When the President of the United States
shall meet the Senate in the Senate chamber, the President of the Senate shall have a chair on the floor, be considered as the head of the

Cherokees to arrange a new boundary; if so, what compensation should be made, and whether the United States should stipulate solemnly to guarantee the new boundary. The Senate by resolution replied to these inquiries in the affirmative.

On January 19, 1791, President Washington laid before the Senate the representation of the chargé d'affaires of France in regard to certain acts of Congress imposing extra tonnage on foreign vessels, and asked the advice of the Senate as to the answer he should make. On February 26, 1791, the Senate, by resolution, replied to this message, stating their opinion as to the meaning of the fifth article of the

Senate, and his chair shall be assigned to the President of the United States."

Rule 35 further provides that: "All questions shall be put by the President of the Senate either in the presence or absence of the President of the United States."

In the revision of the rules adopted January 3, 1820, the provision of Rule 35 in the revision of 1806 was dropped. The provision of rule 34 of 1806 was retained and remained in the Senate rules until 1877, when it was changed to read as follows: "When the President of the United States shall meet the Senate in the Senate chamber for the consideration of executive business, he shall have a seat on the right of the chair." The provision in this form has continued to the present day and is at this time one of the rules of the Senate. Thus it will be seen that although the practice has been given up the original theory of the framers of the Constitution has never been abandoned. The rule of the Senate, now nearly a century old, is a full and significant recognition of the right of the President to consult in person with his constitutional advisers, and of the absolute equality of the Senate and the executive in all matters of executive business in which the Senate shares under the Constitution.

treaty in relation to the acts of Congress which had been called in question, and advising that an answer be given to the chargé d'affaires of France, defending the construction put upon the treaty by the Senate.

On February 14, 1791, a message was sent in which illustrates in a very interesting way how close the relations were between the Senate and the President in all matters relating to treaties, and how completely Washington recognized the right of the Senate to advise with him in regard to every matter connected with our foreign relations. In this message he explained his sending Gouverneur Morris in an unofficial character to England in order to learn whether it were possible to open negotiations for a treaty, and with the message he sent various letters, so that the Senate might be fully informed as to all this business, which was, in its nature, entirely secret and unofficial.

On November 10, 1791, the Senate ratified the treaty made by Governor Blount with the Cherokee Indians, and the report of the committee begins in this way: "That they have examined the said treaty and find it strictly conformable to the instructions given by the President, that these instructions were founded on the advice and consent of the Senate on the 11th of August, 1790," etc.

It is not necessary to multiply instances under our first President. These cases which have been quoted show how Washington interpreted the Constitution which he had so largely helped to frame. It is clear that in his opinion, and in that of the Senate, which does not appear to have been controverted by anybody, the powers of the Senate were exactly equal to those of the President in the making of treaties, and that they were entitled to share with him at all stages of a negotiation.

April 16, 1794, Washington consulted the Senate upon a much more important matter than any of those to which I have referred, for on that day he sent in the name of John Jay to be an envoy extraordinary to England in addition to the minister already there. He gives in the message his reasons for doing this, and in that way caused the Senate to pass not only upon the appointment of Mr. Jay but also upon the policy which that appointment involved.

May 31, 1797, President Adams, in nominating his special commission to France, followed the example of Washington when he nominated Jay, and explained his reasons for the appointment of this commission, in that way taking the advice of the Senate as to opening the negotiations at all.

December 6, 1797, President Adams, in submitting an Indian deed, which was the form taken by the treaty, suggested that it be conditionally ratified; that is, that the Senate should provide that the treaty should not become binding until the President was satisfied as to the investment of the money, and the resolution was put in that form.   This is interesting, because it is the first case where the President himself suggests an amendment to be made by the Senate.

March 6, 1798, in ratifying the treaty with Tunis, where the Senate had made an amendment, they recommended that the President enter into friendly negotiations with the Government of Tunis in regard to the disputed article.

February 6, 1797, President Adams nominated Rufus King minister to Russia, and stated that it was done for the purpose of making a treaty of amity and commerce with that country.

When President Adams re-opened negotiations with France, an action which signalized the fatal breach in the Federalist party, he sent in the name of William Vans Murray to be minister to France, explained that it was to renew the negotiation, and stated further what instructions he should give if Murray was confirmed by the Senate.   So much opposition was aroused by this step that in order to secure the assent of the Senate to his policy Mr. Adams sent in the names of Chief Justice Ellsworth and Patrick Henry to be joined with Murray in the commission, and stated more explicitly the conditions on which alone he would allow them to embark.

President Jefferson, on January 11, 1803, sent in a message nominating Livingston and Monroe to negotiate with France, and Charles Pinckney and Monroe to negotiate with Spain, in regard to Louisiana, setting forth fully his reasons for opening negotiations on this subject, so that the Senate in advising and consenting to the appointments assented also to the policy which they involved.

President Madison, on May 29, 1813, sent in a nomination for a minister to Sweden, to open diplomatic relations with that country. The Senate, on June 14, appointed a committee to confer with the President upon the subject. Madison declined the conference on the ground that a committee could not confer directly with the Executive, but only through a Department. His statement of the relations of the President and Senate in his message of July 6, 1813, is interesting as showing how he, one of the principal framers of the Constitution, construed it in this respect:

Without entering into a general review of the relations in which the Constitution has placed the several departments of the Government to each other, it will suffice to remark that the Executive and Senate, in the cases of appointments to office and of treaties, are to be considered as independent of and co-ordinate with each other. If they agree, the appointments or treaties are made; if the Senate disagree, they fail. If the Senate wish information previous to their final decision, the practice, keeping in view the constitutional relations of the Senate and the Executive, has been either to request the Executive to furnish it or to refer the subject to a committee of their body to communicate, either formally or informally, with the head of the proper Department. The appointment of a committee of the Senate to confer immediately with the Executive himself appears to lose sight of the co-ordinate relation between the Executive and the Senate which the Constitution has established, and which ought therefore to be maintained.

April 6, 1818, President Monroe laid before the Senate correspondence with Great Britain making an arrangement as to naval armaments on the Great Lakes. He asked the Senate to decide whether this was a matter which the Executive was competent to settle alone, and if they thought not, then he asked for their advice and consent to making the agreement.

President Jackson, on March 6, 1829, asked the consent of the Senate to make with the chargé d'affaires of Prussia an exchange of ratifications of the treaty with that country, the time for the exchange having passed before the Prussian ratification was received. The request was repeated on January 26, 1831, under similar circumstances, in regard to the Austrian treaty.[1]

May 6, 1830, President Jackson, in a message relating to a treaty proposed by the Choctaw Indians,

[1] This became the universal practice in cases where the time for exchanging ratifications had expired by accident, or otherwise, before the exchange had been effected. It is not necessary to cite other instances.

16

asked the Senate to share in the negotiations in the following words : " Will the Senate advise the conclusion of a treaty with the Choctaw Nation according to the terms which they propose ? Or will the Senate advise the conclusion of a treaty with that tribe as modified by the alterations suggested by me ? If not, what further alteration or modification will the Senate propose ? " President Jackson then goes on to give his reasons for thus consulting the Senate. The passage is of great interest because it not only states the change of practice which had taken place since Washington's time in regard to consulting the Senate before or during a negotiation, but recognizes fully that although reasons of convenience and expediency had led to the abandonment of consultation with the Senate as a body prior to a negotiation, yet it was an undoubted constitutional right of the President to so consult the Senate, and of the Senate to take part, if it saw fit, at any stage of a negotiation.   President Jackson says :

I am fully aware that in thus resorting to the early practice of the Government, by asking the previous advice of the Senate in the discharge of this portion of my duties, I am departing from a long and for many years unbroken usage in similar cases.   But being satisfied that this resort is consistent with the provisions of the Constitution, that it is strongly recommended in this instance by considerations of expediency, and that the reasons which have led to the observance of a different practice, though very cogent in negotiation with foreign nations, do not apply with equal force to those made with Indian tribes, I flatter myself that it will not meet the disapprobation of the Senate.

Under President John Quincy Adams a convention had been made with Great Britain, referring to the decision of the King of the Netherlands the points of difference between the two nations as to our north-eastern boundary line.   On January 10, 1831, the King of the Netherlands rendered his decision, against which our minister at The Hague protested. On December 7, 1831, President Jackson submitted the decision and protest to the Senate, asking whether they would advise submission to the opinion of the arbiter and consent to its execution.   The President took occasion to say in this connection : " I had always determined, whatever might have been the result of the examination by the sovereign arbiter, to have submitted the same to the Senate for their advice before I executed or rejected it."

On March 3, 1835, the Senate passed the following resolution :

Resolved, That the President of the United States be respectfully requested to consider the expediency of opening negotiations with the governments of other nations, and particularly of the governments of Central America and New Grenada, for the purpose of effectually protecting, by suitable treaty stipulations with them, such individuals or companies as may undertake to open a communication between the Atlantic and Pacific oceans by the construction of a ship canal across the isthmus which connects North and South America, and of securing forever, by such stipulations, the free and equal right of navigating such canal to all such nations, on the payment of such reasonable tolls as may be established, to compensate the capitalists who may engage in such undertaking and complete the work.

January 9, 1837, President Jackson replied to this resolution, stating that in accordance with its terms an agent had been sent to Central America, but that from his report it was apparent that the conditions were not such as to warrant entering upon negotiations for treaties relating to a ship canal.

President Van Buren, on June 7, 1838, sent in a message announcing that he intended to authorize our chargé d'affaires to Peru to go to Ecuador and, as agent of the United States, negotiate a treaty with that Republic. Before doing so, however, he thought it proper, in strict observance of the rights of the Senate, to ask their opinion as to the exercise of such a power by the Executive in opening negotiations and diplomatic relations with a foreign state.

President Polk, on June 10, 1846, sent to the Senate a proposal in the form of a convention in regard to the Oregon boundary submitted by the British minister, together with a protocol of the proceedings, and on this he asked the advice of the

Senate as to what action should be taken. The message then continues as follows:

In the early periods of the Government the opinion and advice of the Senate were often taken in advance upon important questions of our foreign policy. General Washington repeatedly consulted the Senate and asked their previous advice upon pending negotiations with foreign powers, and the Senate in every instance responded to his call by giving their advice, to which he always conformed his action. This practice, though rarely resorted to in later times, was, in my judgment, eminently wise, and may, on occasions of great importance, be properly revived. The Senate are a branch of the treaty-making power, and by consulting them in advance of his own action upon important measures of foreign policy, which may ultimately come before them for their consideration, the President secures harmony of action between that body and himself. The Senate are, moreover, a branch of the war-making power, and it may be eminently proper for the Executive to take the opinion and advice of that body in advance upon any great question which may involve in its decision the issue of peace or war.

August 4, 1846, President Polk, by message, consulted the Senate as to entering upon peace negotiations with Mexico and advancing to that country a portion of the money to be paid as consideration for the cession of territory.

July 28, 1848, President Polk sent to the Senate a message explaining his refusal to ratify an extradition treaty with Prussia, to which the Senate had agreed. When the treaty was sent to the Senate, on December 16, 1845, the President stated his objections to the third article. The Senate ratified the treaty with the third article unamended, and thereupon, and because the Senate had not amended or stricken out the third article, the President refused to ratify the treaty himself.

April 22, 1850, President Taylor invited the Senate to amend either the Clayton-Bulwer treaty or that with Nicaragua, so that they might conform with each other.

February 13, 1852, President Fillmore pointed out certain objectionable clauses in the Swiss treaty and asked the Senate to amend them.

June 26, 1852, President Fillmore sent in a letter from Mr. Webster, calling attention to the non-action of the Senate upon an extradition treaty with Mexico, and asked that, if it was thought objectionable in any particular, amendments might be made to remove the objections, such amendments to be proposed by the Executive to the Mexican Government.

February 10, 1854, President Pierce sent to the Senate the Gadsden treaty, signed by the plenipotentiaries on December 30, 1853, and with it certain amendments which he recommended to the Senate for adoption before ratification. It would be difficult to find a better example than this, not merely of the right of the Senate to amend, but of the fact that Senate amendments are simply a continuance of the negotiation begun by the President.

President Buchanan, on February 12, 1861, asked the advice of the Senate as to accepting the award made by commissioners under the convention with Paraguay, following therein the precedent set by President Jackson.

February 21, 1861, President Buchanan asked the advice of the Senate as to entering into a negotiation with Great Britain for a treaty of arbitration in regard to a controverted point in the Ashburton-Webster treaty of 1846. His own words are : " The precise questions I submit are three : Will the Senate approve a treaty," etc.

March 16, 1861, President Lincoln, in his first message to the Senate, repeated the questions of his predecessor as to entering upon this negotiation for an arbitration with Great Britain, and said : " I find no reason to disapprove the course of my predecessor on this important matter, but, on the contrary, I not only shall receive the advice of the Senate therein, but I respectfully ask the Senate for their advice on the three questions before recited."

December 17, 1861, President Lincoln sent to the Senate a draft of a convention proposed by the Mexican Government, and asked, not for ratification, but merely for their advice upon it.

January 24, 1862, he asked again for advice as
to entering upon the treaty for a loan to Mexico, so
that he might instruct Mr. Corwin in accordance
with the views of the Senate.

February 25, 1862, the Senate passed a resolution to the effect "that it is not advisable to negotiate a treaty that will require the United States
to assume any portion of the principal or interest
of the debt of Mexico, or that will require the
concurrence of European powers." Meantime Mr.
Corwin, not having received instructions, had made
and signed two treaties for the loan, and President
Lincoln, on sending them in on June 23, 1862, said
in his message : " The action of the Senate is, of
course, conclusive against acceptance of the treaties
on my part," but the importance of the subject
was such that he asked for the further advice of
the Senate upon it.

March 5, 1862, President Lincoln sent a message
repeating President Buchanan's request for the
advice of the Senate as to accepting the Paraguayan
award.

February 5, 1863, President Lincoln sent in for
ratification a convention with Peru, and suggested
an amendment which he wished to have made by
the Senate.

January 15, 1869, President Johnson sent in a
protocol agreed upon with Great Britain, and asked

the advice of the Senate as to entering upon a negotiation for a convention based upon the protocol submitted.

April 5, 1871, President Grant transmitted a despatch from our minister to the Hawaiian Islands, and asked for the views of the Senate as to the policy to be pursued.

May 13, 1872, President Grant sent a message to the Senate relating to differences which had arisen under the treaty of Washington, and said : " I respectfully invite the attention of the Senate to the proposed article submitted by the British Government with the object of removing the differences which seem to threaten the prosecution of the arbitration, and request an expression by the Senate of their disposition in regard to advising and consenting to the formal adoption of an article such as is proposed by the British Government.

" The Senate is aware that the consultation with that body in advance of entering into agreements with foreign states has many precedents. In the early days of the Republic, General Washington repeatedly asked their advice upon pending questions with such powers. The most important recent precedent is that of the Oregon boundary treaty, in 1846.

" The importance of the results hanging upon the present state of the treaty with Great Britain leads me to follow these former precedents, and to desire the counsel of the Senate in advance of agreeing to the proposal of Great Britain."

June 18, 1874, President Grant sent in a draft of a reciprocity treaty relating to Canada, and asked the Senate if they would concur in such a treaty if negotiated.

President Arthur, on June 9, 1884, asked the advice of the Senate as to directing negotiations to proceed with the King of Hawaii for the extension of the existing reciprocity treaty with the Hawaiian Islands.

March 3, 1888, the Senate passed a resolution asking President Cleveland to open negotiations with China for the regulation of immigration with that country. President Cleveland replied that such negotiations had been undertaken.

From these various examples it will be seen that the Senate has been consulted at all stages of negotiations by Presidents of all parties, from Washington to Arthur. It will also be observed that the right to recommend a negotiation by resolution was exercised in 1835 and again in 1888, and was unquestioned by either Jackson or Cleveland, who were probably more unfriendly to the Senate and more unlikely to accede to any extension of Senate prerogatives than any Presidents we have ever had. It will be further noted that the Senate in 1862

advised against the Mexican negotiation, and that
President Lincoln frankly accepted their decision,
and did not even ask that the treaties which had
been actually made meantime should be considered
with a view to ratification.

The power of the Senate to amend or to ratify
conditionally is of course included in the larger
powers expressly granted by the Constitution to
reject or confirm. It would have never occurred
to me that any one who had read the Constitution
and who possessed even the most superficial acquaintance with the history of the United States
could doubt the right of the Senate to amend. But
within the last year[1] I have seen this question raised,
not jocosely, so far as one could see, but quite seriously. It may be well, therefore, to point out very
briefly the law and the facts as to the power of
the Senate to amend or alter treaties.

In 1795 the Senate amended the Jay treaty, ratifying it on condition that the twelfth article should
be suspended. Washington accepted their action
without a word of comment, as if it were a matter
of course, and John Marshall, in his Life of Washington, has treated the Senate's action on that
memorable occasion in the same way. From that
day to this, from the Jay treaty in 1795 to the alien
property treaty with Great Britain in 1900, the

[1] 1900–1901.

Senate has amended treaties, and foreign governments, recognizing our system and the propriety of the Senate's action, have accepted the amendments. A glance at the passages which have been cited from the Messages of the Presidents is enough to disclose the fact that no President has ever questioned the right of the Senate to amend, and that several Presidents have invited the Senate to make amendments as the best method of continuing the negotiations. In this case, however, we are not left to deduce the obvious right of the Senate to amend, from an unbroken line of precedents and the unquestioning recognition of the right by the Chief Executive. On this point we have a direct and unanimous declaration by the Supreme Court of the United States. In Haver v. Yaker, Mr. Justice Davis, delivering the opinion of the court, said: " In this country a treaty is something more than a contract, for the Federal Constitution declares it to be the law of the land. If so, before it can become a law, the Senate, in whom rests the authority to ratify it, must agree to it. But the Senate are not required to adopt or reject it as a whole, but may modify or amend it, as was done with the treaty under consideration." [1] This decision of the court is conclusive,

[1] Wallace, pp. 34 and 35. Mr. Rawle, in his " View of the Constitution of the United States," p. 64, says: " The Senate may

if any doubt had ever existed as to the amendment powers of the Senate; but the following list of treaties, amended by the Senate and afterwards ratified by the countries with which they were made, exhibits the uniform and unquestioned practice which has prevailed since the foundation of our Government :

Algiers, 1795; Argentine, 1885 (amity and commerce), 1897 (extradition) ; Austria, 1856; Baden, 1857; Bavaria, 1845, 1853; Belgium, 1858, 1880 (consular); Bolivia, 1859, 1900 (extradition) ; Brunswick and Luneburg, 1854; Chile, 1900 (extradition); China, 1868, 1887 (exclusion); Colombia, 1857; New Granada, 1888 (extradition); Congo, 1891 (relations); Costa Rica, 1852, 1861; France, 1778, 1843, 1858, 1886 (claims), 1892 (extradition); Great Britain, 1794, 1815, 1889 (extradition), 1891 (Bering Sea), 1896 (Bering claims), 1899 (real property) ; Guatemala, 1870 (amity and commerce); Hawaii, 1875 (reciprocity), 1886 (reciprocity); Italy, 1868; Japan, 1886 (extradition), 1894 (extradition), 1894 (commerce and navigation); Mexico, 1843, 1848, 1853, 1861, 1868, 1883 (reciprocity), 1885 (reciprocity), 1886 (boundary), 1888 (frontier), 1890 (boundary); Netherlands, 1887 (extradition) ; Nicaragua, 1859, 1870 (amity and commerce) ; Orange Free State,

wholly reject it, or they may ratify it in part, or recommend additional or explanatory articles, which, if the President approves of them, again become the subject of negotiation between him and the foreign power; and, finally, when the whole receives the consent of the Senate, and the ratifications are exchanged between the respective Governments, the treaty becomes obligatory on both nations." Mr. Rawley's entire chapter on the treaty-making power merits careful consideration in this connection.

1896 (extradition); Peru, 1863, 1887 (commerce and navigation), 1899 (extradition); Russia, 1889 (extradition); Saxony, 1845; Siam, 1856; Sweden, 1816, 1869 (naturalization); Switzerland, 1847, 1850, 1900 (extradition); Tunis, 1797, Turkey, 1830, 1874 (extradition); Two Sicilies, 1855; Venezuela, 1886 (claims).

From this list it appears that there have been 68 treaties amended by the Senate and afterwards ratified.

The results of the preceding inquiry can be easily summarized. Practice and precedent, the action of the Senate and of the Presidents, and the decision of the Supreme Court show that the power of the Senate in making treaties has always been held, as the Constitution intended, to be equal to and coordinate with that of the President, except in the initiation of a negotiation, which can of necessity only be undertaken by the President alone. The Senate has the right to recommend entering upon a negotiation, or the reverse; but this right it has wisely refrained from exercising, except upon rare occasions. The Senate has the right to amend, and this right it has always exercised largely and freely. It is also clear that any action taken by the Senate is a part of the negotiation, just as much so as the action of the President through the Secretary of State. In other words, the action of the Senate upon a treaty is not merely to give sanction to the treaty, but is an integral part of the treaty making, and may be taken at any stage of a negotiation.

It has been frequently said of late that the Senate in the matter of treaties has been extending its powers and usurping rights which do not properly belong to it. That the power of the Senate has grown during the past century is beyond doubt, but it has not grown at all in the matter of treaties. On the contrary, the Senate now habitually leaves in abeyance rights as to treaty-making which at the beginning of the Government it freely exercised, and it has shown in this great department of executive government both wisdom and moderation in the assertion of its constitutional powers.

This is not the place to discuss the abstract merits of the constitutional provisions as to the making of treaties. Under a popular government like ours it would be neither possible nor safe to leave the vast powers of treaty-making exclusively in the hands of a single person. Some control over the Executive in this regard must be placed in the Congress, and the framers of the Constitution intrusted it to the representatives of the States. That they acted wisely cannot be questioned, even if the requirement of the two-thirds vote for ratification is held to be a too narrow restriction. These, however, are considerations of no practical importance, and after all only concern ourselves. Our system of treaty-making is established by the Constitution and has been made clear by long practice and uniform precedents. The American people understand it, and those who conduct the government of other countries are bound to understand it, too, when they enter upon negotiations with us. There is no excuse for any misapprehension. It is well also that the representatives of other nations should remember, whether they like our system or not, that in the observance of treaties during the last one hundred and twenty-five years there is not a nation in Europe which has been so exact as the United States, nor one which has a record so free from examples of the abrogation of treaties at the pleasure of one of the signers alone.

SOME IMPRESSIONS OF RUSSIA

SOMEWHAT more than a year ago [1] Eduard Suess, the distinguished Austrian geologist, eminent alike in science and in public life, celebrated his seventieth birthday. To a gathering of his friends who had waited upon him to present their congratulations, he made an address in which he discussed the political and economic future of the nations of the earth. The theme was very appropriate to the speaker, for modern history in these latest days has been engaged in demonstrating more and more surely and clearly that the discovery, possession, and development of mineral deposits have played always a leading and often a controlling part in the rise and fall of states and empires, in the growth and decay of civilizations, and in the movements of trade and the accumulation of wealth. This phase of history was, therefore, the one naturally taken by Herr Suess for his text, and in the course of his discussion he is reported to have said that, owing to their mineral resources, the future belonged to three nations, — the United States, Russia, and China, but with a long interval between the first and second ; and that the supremacy of the nations

---

[1] This article was published in Scribner's Magazine for April, 1902.

17

of western Europe and of England was over, because
their natural resources, heavily drawn upon for many
centuries, and never very large, were rapidly approaching exhaustion. To the geologist a thousand
years are, indeed, but as yesterday, and that which
he speaks of as immediate frequently seems to the
average man extremely remote. Many years, no
doubt, must elapse before the mineral resources of
England and western Europe actually give out or
become unprofitable from difficulty in working. Yet
the end is pressing sufficiently close to cause England and Europe to watch the progress of the United
States with an interest hitherto unknown, and which,
whether it finds expression in serious discussion, in
sneers, or in denunciations, is none the less real and
none the less tremulous with apprehension of the
rival at whom they have been wont to scoff. We, on
the other hand, do not fret ourselves overmuch about
the nations we are overtaking and passing in the
race for trade, commerce, and economic supremacy.
We observe all they do, with much care, but without
anxiety. To us the great country placed next behind
us by the geologist is a subject of keener interest,
although no cause for present fear. It is true that,
owing to the superior energy of the American people,
a long interval still separates us from Russia, in the
prediction of Herr Suess. But none the less Russia
has the natural resources, — she has, like ourselves, a

large future; her natural resources are still undeveloped. The nations which have hitherto held economic supremacy, but whose natural resources have
begun to contract and decline, demand, no doubt,
our most watchful attention, but need not excite un-
due apprehension. Ultimate peril, if there is any,
can only come from a nation of the future, with possibilities as yet unmeasured and unknown.

To every reflecting American, therefore, Russia is
of absorbing interest, not only on account of the
friendship she has frequently shown us, but because
she is potentially an economic rival more formidable
than any other organized nation. We know that
somewhere in that vast territory which extends from
the Baltic to the Pacific and from the Arctic Ocean
to the Black Sea, there is found every variety of
soil and climate and every kind of mineral wealth.
The coal, the iron, the gold, and the copper may not
be so compactly or so conveniently placed as in the
United States, but they are all there. That which it
concerns us to know is how far this great country
and its resources are now developed, whether they
can be fully and effectively developed by the Russian
people, and, if so, how soon they will reach the point
of dangerous and destructive rivalry. These were
the questions to which I sought reply when I
travelled in Russia last summer;[1] and on the prin-

[1] The summer of 1901.

ciple of seeking and finding, I received a number of very vivid impressions which seemed to furnish in some degree answers to the questions I had in mind. I shall try here to set down certain of those impressions, with the hope that they may help us to understand the present and gauge the future conditions with some accuracy, for upon our knowledge of these conditions our success in the great economic struggle, upon which we have entered so victoriously and so cheerfully, largely depends.

We came into Russia from Vienna by way of Poland, and stopped at Warsaw. Here was a large city full of business activity, curiously devoid of any sign of age more remote than the days of " Augustus, the Physically Strong," and with new quarters which closely resembled Chicago. Everywhere there was bustle, life, energy ; very clearly an economic people with abundant capacity for the competition of the present time. And over this large, thriving, moving, rather commonplace community lies ever the shadow of 80,000 armed men, for that is the garrison needed, apparently, to maintain the peace for which Warsaw has become proverbial. The people are Polish and Jewish, the soldiers are Russians. In other words, the economic people here are not Russians, and their obvious capacity for modern business throws no light upon Russia unless by way of contrast. But from another point of view the relative positions of the two races are full of instruction, and embody very strikingly the great truth that economic capacity is futile unless it is sustained by the nobler abilities which enable a people to rule and administer and to display that social efficiency in war, peace, and government without which all else is vain. It is well worth while to pause a moment as one looks at Warsaw, and remember how great a part the Poles have played in history. They were the barrier of Europe against the Turk. Only three centuries ago they were in Moscow, pulling down and setting up Tsars. They were, and are, a gallant people, brilliant in war, versatile, clever, interesting. They were, and are, far cleverer, far more attractive, far quicker than the Russians; but they were unable to govern themselves or others, and the Russians have shown themselves able to do both. They were anarchic, weakly unable to combine and to make sacrifices for a common end. The Russians were orderly, organized, concentrated. One is irresistibly reminded by Poland of Bagehot's famous proposition that in great governing races there is always a certain amount of stupidity, and that "while the Romans were prætors, the Greeks were barbers," — an illustration which he might have supplemented by one equally apt, drawn from contemporary Warsaw. But none the less, however we may explain it, and however much we may dislike the political system and methods by which Poland is controlled, the fact remains that the Russians govern Poland, which could not govern itself, as well as much other vast territory and many other hostile or alien peoples. We may object to their way of doing it, but we must concede at the outset that the Russians have the governing capacity, without which no race and no nation can aspire to political power or hope for material success. The manner may be harsh, but the Russians can maintain order, with which failure is likely enough, but without which nothing is possible, except anarchy and chaos, hateful above all things to gods and men and Thomas Carlyle.

The railroad from Warsaw to Moscow follows almost exactly the route of Napoleon and the Grand Army. The country is still the same as in his day, except for the railroad itself; and as the dreary plain, broken only by vast stretches of monotonous birch and pine forests, slips by, hour after hour and mile after mile, the greatness of the man who crossed it with an army looms ever larger on the imagination. The military genius of Napoleon seems more marvellous than ever before, while the lone and level plain, the marshes, the woods, the chill and sluggish rivers, silent witnesses of his great march, stare back at the gazer as the train runs slowly onward. It was this same country that destroyed his army on its retreat after the ruinous and inexplicable delay at Moscow which insured a defeat that could have been so easily avoided. The victory of the desolate wind-swept plains over the only soldier of modern times worthy to rank with Cæsar, Alexander, and Hannibal suggests some interesting reflections. The Russians have expanded their borders and added to their possessions more than any people in modern times, except those who speak English. The Tsar holds sway to-day over a territory as compact as the United States and more than twice as large. Throwing out the Arctic wastes of Canadian North America, Russia in Europe and Asia has nearly as large an area as that of all the widely scattered British possessions. Yet it was not until late in the sixteenth century, less than four hundred years ago, that Russia finally shook herself free from Tartar dominion. Two hundred more years elapsed before her political organization became consolidated and coherent, free from the intermeddling of Poles and Swedes. Her great extension of territory has practically taken place within two hundred years; that is, since the accession of Peter the Great. When it is remembered that the world movement of the English-speaking people began nearly a hundred years earlier, with the first settlement of America and the opening of the East India trade, the length and rapidity of the strides Russia has made in the acquisition of territory and the spread of her empire can be quickly appreciated.

Yet a very conspicuous fact about Russian history is that she has never been a conquering nation, in the usual military sense. She has never swept, swift and victorious, over vast spaces of the earth, like the Tartar hordes which held her in bondage for two hundred and fifty years, and whose scattered remnants are now her peaceful subjects. Her best known successes in war have been, as a rule, defensive victories, where country and climate were the allies of her soldiers, as when she ruined Charles, of Sweden, at Pultava, or destroyed the Grand Army of Napoleon, pursuing his retreating columns over snow and ice, more deadly and destructive than all her soldiers and artillery. She has steadily pushed back the Turks in many wars of varying fortune, but the empire has not been made by military conquerors of the type of Alexander or Cæsar or Napoleon. Suvaroff, alone, had large success in the offensive, outside his own country, and after his recall the Russian army was beaten by Massena at Zurich.

The Russians, indeed, have not been over-successful in war. They have always fought with dogged stubbornness, but military genius seems to have been lacking. It is true that they have slowly driven back the Turks, and yet in their very last war Turkey, crippled as she was, inflicted many bloody repulses upon them and stayed the march to Constantinople. Nevertheless, with the exception of the

English-speaking race, no people have acquired territory so rapidly and steadily, or held it more firmly. No matter what checks they have received, the Russian movement has gone persistently forward. They have spread to the Baltic on the north and to the Black Sea on the south. They have crossed the Urals and carried their empire to the Pacific. Even now they are grasping Manchuria and have opened their way to the Persian Gulf, despite the fact that England, if we may believe Captain Mahan, has been increasing her prestige and improving her military strength in South Africa. They hold Poland, Finland, and the German Baltic provinces in an unwilling but complete subjection. They have brought the Cossacks, that wild blend of Tartar and Greek with outlawed Poles and Russians, to an entire and satisfactory loyalty, while the still wilder tribes of Central Asia accept their dominion quietly, and rest content under their rule. The people of the South and East, with a less advanced civilization, welcome Russian government, while those of the western border, more civilized and more intelligent than their masters, detest it, but both alike are held quiet and submissive in an iron grip. Here, then, is a nation which has shown two great and vital qualities of an imperial and ruling race, — the ability to govern and the ability to expand and conquer, as well as to consolidate and hold its conquests.

Twenty years ago it would have been admitted unquestioningly that a nation with such attributes and such achievements in the recent past must soon become, not only a portentous rival to all other nations, but that, except for some very unforeseen contingency, it was certain to attain to supremacy, if not to absolute domination in the affairs of the world. Since that time, however, a new school of historians has arisen, of which Mr. Brooks Adams, in his "Law of Civilization and Decay," was the pioneer and first exponent, and which has set forth and sustained the theory that the rise and fall of states and civilizations, nations and races, are governed by processes of evolution as sure as those applied by Darwin to the world of nature, and less definite only because our knowledge of the highly complicated facts is inferior and our opportunities of observation more limited. This new school further holds with Karl Marx that in these processes of evolution the controlling forces, in ancient and modern times alike, have been economic. This doctrine, if carried to extremes, may easily become as misleading as any other; for the one thing absolutely certain about human history is that, in the infinite complications of human motives and passions, no single theory and no one simple truth can alone explain all the doings of mankind and all the events of the past. The economic forces

have been so utterly overlooked hitherto, and have
really played such a great and, at times, dominant
part in the history of mankind, that it is easy in
reaction against their undeserved neglect to go too
far with them. Properly understood, they give light
in many places where before there was darkness;
they often show continuity, where hitherto blind
chance seemed to reign; they demonstrate the processes of evolution and they explain much, but taken
alone they do not explain everything. A nation
may produce great economic capacity, and yet fail.
Even the towering genius of Hannibal could not
save the Carthaginians, a race of high economic
ability, from defeat by a people at that time of
low economic capacity, but endowed with greater
tenacity of purpose, greater ability to stand punish-
ment, and superior quality in war. The Huns swept
over Europe in conquest and disappeared, for they
had neither organizing, administrative, nor economic
capabilities. The nation which can only fight, no
matter how brilliantly, will not endure. Like Hun
and Tartar, it will go down. The nation which is
purely economic, no matter how much it wins in
commerce or how vast the wealth it piles up, cannot
long survive ; for some fighting people whom it
has beaten in trade will destroy it in war. Carthage
fell before the advance of Rome. A people may
combine fighting and economic qualities, and yet

break down because they cannot organize and govern. Poland furnishes a sad example of such a case. A nation may be able to fight, trade, and organize, and yet, if unable to expand and spread, will not endure. Spain rose to domination under her statesmen and soldiers, and was brought to the ground by Holland, grotesquely unequal as an antagonist, because Holland could not only fight desperately, but by marvellous economic talents turned the tide of wealth to Amsterdam and ruined her mighty foe, who could not make, but could only spend, money. The Dutch in turn failed to expand, and after a period of great power dropped out of the race and lost their place among the leading nations.

It is not enough, therefore, that a nation should have shown, as Russia has shown, the power to conquer territory, to fight, govern, and expand. She must also prove that she is gifted with the economic qualities, never so essential as now when the economic forces are more relentless and controlling than ever before in history. Does she possess these qualities, or can she develop them? On the answer to these questions her future depends. To seek to make this momentous answer complete would be a life-work for one man; and when the life had been given, the task would probably remain unfinished. But indications of the right reply, foundations for just conclusions, contributions to the final settlement of the problem, these can be gathered everywhere, in the history of the past, in the facts and statistics of the present; they can even be discovered in the first vivid impressions of the passing traveller, if he will take the trouble to look at the scenes and people before him with considerate eyes, and formulate what he perceives, so that it shall be intelligible to others.

To a native of western Europe or of the United States, the first feeling which masters him in Russia is that he has come among a people whose fundamental ideas, whose theory of life, and whose controlling motives of action are utterly alien to his own. There is no common ground, no common starting-place, no common premise of thought and action. The fact that the Russians on the surface and in external things are like us, only accentuates the underlying and essential differences. In all the outward forms of social life, in the higher education, in methods of intercourse both public and private, they do not differ from us, and Peter's imitative policy has in all these things been carried to completion. That the man in the breech-clout, that the wearer of the turban or the pigtail, should be wholly alien to us is so obvious that we are not startled. But that men who in the world of society and in the cities dress like us and have our manners should be at bottom so utterly different, gives a sharp and emphatic jar to all one's preconceived ideas.

It is always difficult to state in few words the radical differences which separate one people from another in thought and habits, in the conduct and ideals of life. But here the past helps us to a definition at once broad and suggestive. We are the children of Rome, and the Russians are the children of Byzantium. Between Rome, republican or imperial, and its Greek successor at Byzantium there was a great gulf fixed. One was Latin, the other was the Greek of decadence and subjection. One was Western, the other was Eastern. Ideas inherited from Rome permeated western Europe and were brought thence to America. From Rome comes our conception of patriotism, to take but a single example, that love of country which made Rome what she was in her great days. The patriotism of the Russian applies only to the Tsar. In Glinka's fine and most characteristic opera, "A Life for the Tsar," the old peasant who saves his sovereign has no word for Russia, but only for the Tsar. Give your life, give everything for the Tsar! is his cry; and the songs which move the audience to profound excitement are passionate appeals ending in prayer to sacrifice all for the preservation of the Tsar. That which stirs an American, an Englishman, a Frenchman, or a German to heroic deeds is devotion to his native land, to his fatherland, to that ideal entity which is known as " country." That which moves the Russian is devotion to a man who, next to God, commands his religious faith and stands to him for his country. The first conception is Roman, and of the Western World. The second is Oriental, and pertains to the subtle Greek intellect in its decadence. Nor is this feeling the personal loyalty of the Cavalier and the Jacobite to the Stuarts, or of the French *noblesse* to the house of Bourbon. The loyalty of the Russian is not to Alexander or to Nicholas or to the Romanoffs, a family of mixed blood, chiefly German and less than three hundred years ago of the rank of boyars. The intense Russian loyalty is to the crowned and consecrated Tsar, whoever he may be, the head of the State and the head of the Church, next to God in their prayers. Superadded to the deep religious feeling for the Tsar is that due to the fact that when Peter came to the throne commerce and industry belonged to the Tsar, like everything else, and in the words of Peter's latest biographer, Waliszewski, " The Tsar is not only master, he is, in the most absolute sense of the word, proprietor of his country and his people." Whatever changes or modifications came from the " great reformer," or have come since, have been in details. The great central idea that the Tsar not only represents God on earth, but that he owns country and people, is still dominant and controlling. In other words, the State, in the person of the Tsar, is owner and master, and the result is a military and religious socialism which is economically a wasteful and clumsy system, utterly unable to compete against the intense individualism of other countries working through highly perfected and economical organizations.

The same difference of feeling as to the relations of men may be seen in everything. The religious obeisance of the Russians, for example, with its crouching attitude and the head touching the pavement, is thoroughly Oriental, and never was known in any Western Church. One feels at every step the great gulf fixed between those who inherit the ideas of Roman law, liberty, and patriotism, and those who still hold to the slavish doctrines of the Greek Empire of Byzantium.

In the famous opera of Glinka, which has just been mentioned, one catches, indeed, the keynote of the Russian system. The hero is not a prince or a boyar or a victorious general, but a simple moujik, and the other great figure is the Tsar, who never appears on the stage at all, but upon whose fate the entire play turns. The moujik is Russia, and on the moujik rests the government of the Tsar. So long as the moujik remains as he is, the Russian autocracy can neither be touched nor shaken. The outbreaks of Nihilists and students are mere froth upon the surface of society. While the moujik fills the army and believes in the Tsar, all the efforts of the discontented and the agitators are as vain and empty as the passing wind.[1]

But as the moujik is Russia, it is on him and his qualities that not only the government, but the future of the country depends. Is he able to take a successful part in the economic competition of the time? If he is, Russia will succeed, and the most prosperous and powerful of nations may dread the rivalry. If he is not, Russia will ultimately fail. It is true that in the Finns and the Poles, in the Germans of the Baltic Provinces and the Tartars of the South — remnants of the hordes which once held the country to tribute — we have industrial and economic people capable of economic development, and even now largely in possession of the business and capital of the empire. But these outlying races are in a hopeless minority, and, with the exception of the Tartars, they, in various degrees, detest their masters; they have no control, and never will have: in a word, they are not Rus-

[1] The serious indication in the recent disorders in Russia is that workingmen and peasants have been involved, and that in certain cases the soldiers have shown signs of revolt. If these symptoms spread and become general, it will show that the moujik is at last affected, and then and not till then great changes will come.

sian and the spirit and soul of Russia are not in them. There is no need to waste time over them. If we would try to read, however dimly, the future of Russia, we must look to the Russian alone, and really to the Russian moujik; for the educated upper class, cultivated into an external imitation of western Europe, are not Russia, and have power and meaning only when they represent and are in close accord with the vast inert mass of the population beneath them, as was the case alike with the Russian Peter and the German Catherine, the two great rulers and builders of the empire.

What does the moujik reveal, then, to the eyes of the passing traveller? I saw him and his country first, as we slowly crossed the vast plain which lies between Warsaw and Moscow. In that long, monotonous stretch of eight hundred miles, one notes that there are only three cities of any size, — Minsk, with 91,000 inhabitants; Brest-Litovsk, with 48,000; and Smolensk, with 46,000. There are only six towns, including these three, of over 10,000 inhabitants, and only nine with more than 5,000. This is an old part of the empire, some of the cities having been important in the Middle Ages, but there has been no industrial growth, no concentration of labor and capital, no organization like that of the West. Yet the country is all occupied. The farming villages appear at intervals. They are composed of log houses huddled together, tumble-down, dirty, the chinks stuffed with clay. They closely resemble the worst cabins of the early American pioneers which gave place to the clapboarded or brick house in a generation, so quickly, indeed, that except in the region of the negro and in remote districts they have largely disappeared from our Southern and Western country in the course of a century's advance. But the Russians have not advanced beyond the log-cabin stage in eight hundred years. In some of the larger villages one sees occasionally two or three houses sheathed in boards and looking like an American frame house, but these are the exceptions. It is true that Russia is a country of wood and without building stone, but they could build frame houses, and they have abundance of brick-clay. Yet there they are in the rudest pioneer stage in this long-settled region (Moscow was nearly all wood less than two hundred years ago), and there they have remained in rural districts, while the centuries have slipped by unheeded. The eager desire for improvement in material condition, so characteristic of the people who settled the United States, seems to be lacking in the Russian peasant, for even the most adverse circumstances could not account for such widespread absence of progress. Such immobility cannot arise from outside causes, but must have its roots deep down in the nature of the race.

Even more striking than the primitive character of the villages is the absence of roads, of which, in White Russia, at least, there are apparently none better than casual cart-tracks. One can hardly believe, as the watch indicates approach to the journey's end, that the train is drawing near a great capital of a million inhabitants and a thousand years old. The blank, roadless plain goes on up to the edge of Moscow, which has no suburbs; and even when one drives to a pleasure-resort only five miles from the city, that which passes for a road would be thought bad in the most remote mountain districts of the southern Alleghanies. One is also struck in this part of Russia by the absence of any improved implements of agriculture. A horse-plough is the only advance made over hand labor, the reaping, gleaning, and threshing all being done by hand and chiefly by women and girls, the men being largely away in the army or earning money in the cities as cabmen or laborers or in small and simple industries. In southern Russia American agricultural machinery has been introduced and is extensively used; but White Russia, lying between Warsaw and Moscow, is apparently destitute of such improvements, although its inferiority of soil and vast extent of arable land render improved methods of cultivation peculiarly necessary, from the economic point of view.

Far stronger, however, than any impression received from the villages or farms as to the nature of the Russian is that conveyed by his religious attitude. Watch the people at church during some of its noble and always imposing ceremonies, at the shrines of saints or in the holy places of the Kremlin on a feast-day, and you recognize at once that you are in the presence of a religious faith of a kind unknown to western Europe and to America, whether Roman Catholic or Protestant. Here one feels at once that he is in contact with a faith very touching and beautiful to see, which never reasons and has never recognized reason or sought even to dispute its arguments. The devotion is simple, blind, and so unquestioning that the onlooker of another creed finds no intolerance apparent anywhere, and never is disposed to think that the forms so sedulously observed are in the least perfunctory or mechanical among the mass of the people. It is the extreme faith of the Middle Ages in full life, but without the ferocity, the blind fears, or the asceticism which disfigured that period in western Europe. While the Russian people hold to their present faith, the Tsar, who is part of their worship and belief, has an authority founded on a rock which nothing can shake. The hero of Glinka's opera, the scene of which is laid in the seventeenth century, wears the dress of the First Crusade; and however glaring the anachronism historically, the sentiment is true of Russia to-day and always, for the faith of the people is of the time of the crusaders, and could be stimulated even now to similar outbreaks.

The question which confronts those who try to read the future is, what effect will religious faith of this kind have ultimately in the struggle of the present day? We know that when the darkness of the Middle Ages broke, when our ancestors again discovered themselves and the world, when they read once more in the story of ancient times what civilization had been, the dominion of fear passed away, and the economic forces rose again out of their long twilight, and assumed their pristine influence in states and empires. We know that the nations which most thoroughly and readily adapted themselves to the changed conditions climbed most quickly to wealth and power, and those who failed in adaptation went to the wall. France, Germany, Holland, and, above all, the English-speaking people pushed to the front and strove for supremacy. The Spaniard, nearest to-day to the mediæval man and least able to meet the new demands, sank steadily until he lost even his great qualities of war and statecraft which had made the vast empire of Charles V., and so went down in hopeless wreck. The Spaniards were an old people, who were unable to survive as a great power in new conditions. The Russians are a new people so far as Western civilization is concerned, but the inexorable economic forces are upon them now, and they must meet them or fall back. It may be asked what practical effect the religion of the Russians has, economically speaking. Two examples will suffice. The Russian calendar is a fortnight behindhand, and is a constant annoyance, disturbance, and hindrance to the conduct of commerce. The Government is anxious to bring Russian dates into harmony with facts and with the rest of the world, but does not dare to do so because popular feeling would be outraged by dropping a fortnight, which would efface in one year some saints' days and feast-days and would disarrange the rest. When Peter changed the Russian date from the year 7208, dating from the creation of the world, to 1700 A. D., bold as he was he did not dare to accept the Gregorian Calendar, and among his many reforms this partial one required as much audacity as any. The same feeling which Peter thus outraged exists to-day as strongly as ever, and the Russian will not sacrifice to business convenience a sentiment about the calendar of no real moment whatever to his faith or his religion.

This feeling for the existing calendar grows from the profound popular reverence and affection for the saints' days and holy-days, and here the effect in practical affairs is much more marked. In addition to the fifty-two Sundays, Russia has about thirty-nine holidays or feast-days of the Church. They are kept as rigidly almost as a London Sunday. Business ceases, except in nooks and corners, while drunkenness, the bane of the Russian, cripples work for twenty-four or forty-eight hours after each feast. In round numbers, there are thirty days on which the Western World works while the Russian stands idle. Consider the enormous production of thirty days in the United States alone; look at the statistics, and you realize at once that in this single point Russia labors under a wellnigh hopeless disadvantage.

But the matter of holidays is but a single concrete example of a state of mind. Far more serious and deep-rooted is the mental attitude of the men who make and who are the Russian Empire, who sustain the great military and religious socialism which that empire really is, toward the principles of business which are not merely the truisms, but the ordinary instincts of the Western nations. Two little anecdotes will illustrate my meaning.

A secretary of embassy took a house one summer outside St. Petersburg, and, driving to the station the first day, when he paid the driver his twenty-five kopecks, said: " I shall go into St. Petersburg and come out daily now for a month, and I should like to make an arrangement with you to take me back and forth from the station every day."

The reply was prompt: "If I am to take you back and forth from the station every day I shall have to charge you more than twenty-five kopecks, which you paid me for a single trip this morning."

Again, a foreign minister was in the habit of having books bound two or three at a time. Just before his departure he wished to have some fifty books bound in the same way; sent for the binder and asked him at what price he would bind fifty volumes. The reply was: "If you are going to have as many as fifty bound, I shall have to charge you more per volume than for two or three."

It may be said these are isolated instances, but they are none the less typical of a mental attitude among the masses of the people upon economic questions which is suggestive in the highest degree. It is safe to say that it would be impossible to find a huckster in the streets of London, Paris, or New York who would not at once, and instinctively, make a reduction in price to any one who would buy a quantity instead of a single one of his petty wares. The same ignorance of the simplest laws of successful business runs through everything in Russia, from the use of beads strung on wires to count with in the shops and banks, to the clumsy fee system for the payment of public officials.

When one passes from the habits and customs which can be easily noted by the observant travel-

ler, to the broad facts open to all who will
study books, statistics, and economic development,
the indications furnished in the daily life of the
people receive a profound and startling confirmation. Take, for example, the railroad system, probably
more vital to national success, in the conditions of
the present day, than any other single element.
When George Stephenson devised the locomotive
and railroads began, it was as open to Russia as to
any other country to develop railways in the empire,
but now, nearly three-quarters of a century after
Stephenson's day, Russia, with more than 8,000,000
square miles of territory, has barely 35,000 miles
of railway, while the United States, with 3,000,000
square miles of territory, excluding Alaska, has
200,000 miles.[1] It would be difficult to find a
stronger expression of the comparative economic
energy of two great nations than is conveyed by
this single and striking example. One sees constantly in the magazines articles, especially by
English writers, expressing the most profound admiration at the completion of the Siberian Railway,
and yet nothing could be more convincing of the

---

[1] The Almanach de Gotha for 1902 gives the railroad mileage of
Russia as follows :

Russia in Europe	28,042 miles
Russia in Asia	4,710 miles
Finland	1,757 miles

The " United States Railway Gazette " estimates the railway mileage of the United States at the present time as 199,378 miles.

very low economic force of Russia than that same railroad. That it is an important work, that it will help Russia in the East, both economically and for military purposes, cannot be questioned, and yet to wonder at the building of the Trans-Siberian Railroad is only possible if we fail to look below the surface.

Russia has been occupied for more than ten years in building 6,000 miles of railway over a very easy country for the most part, and that railway is not yet completed. The turn around Lake Baikal, which involves serious difficulties, is not yet made, and will not be for some years. The Manchurian branch is not yet complete. But assume that we may call the railway completed, what do we find? It has taken Russia ten years to build 6,000 miles of railroad. The annual construction of railways in the United States has twice reached 6,000 miles. The Russian road has cost in the easiest part $30,000 a mile, and in Siberia it has probably cost, with the equipment, $50,000 a mile. Yet, despite this enormous and wasteful expenditure, they have only got a single track laid with rails so light that they must relay it from one end to the other. It is as yet a complete failure commercially. It is not paying its expenses. If it was a private corporation it would have gone into bankruptcy. It has been paid for in loans which have helped to sink Russia in debt, and is maintained out of taxes imposed upon the people. In one year the people of the United States, by private enterprise, without any aid from the Government or without any taxes upon the people, have built as much as Russia has built in ten years, and most of it is profitable and has been constructed at a cost which would make Russian competition commercially impossible. The Trans-Siberian Railroad, when its statistics are examined, is a most startling exhibition of economic inefficiency.

There is no need here to enter into a discussion of the general economic condition of Russia. The railroads alone tell the story. They are totally inadequate to the business of the country. Most of them have been laid for a military or strategic purpose, and this has thrown many of the industrial towns of Russia out of the line of communication and has made them eccentric. This meagre railway system is also totally inadequate for distribution or transportation. Famines recur yearly in different parts of Russia, and yet the total wheat crop is more than enough to feed her whole people, but the means of transportation make intercommunication and relief impossible.

The truth is that the Russians are a primitive people, and at the same time an old people; that is, they have been long established in their present territory. It is important to remember these two facts, because it shows that they have not been able to grow out of their primitive ideas during a long period of time, which indicates that they are, as a people, incapable of the economic advancement or of the adaptation to modern conditions by which alone they can hope to survive and win ultimate success in the struggle. A primitive people is economically wasteful, and the Russian system is wasteful and inefficient to the last degree. With a vast country and unlimited resources, the problem before Russia is that of development. Can they develop the enormous property which is theirs? Thus far they have failed to do so, except in a comparatively slight degree, and there is no present indication that they will be able to develop their country with their existing methods. It would be rash to say of any people that they cannot be turned into an economic and industrial nation, especially when they are as patient, docile, stubborn of courage, and tenacious of purpose as the Russians; but it is certain that it would take many generations to bring this about with the Russians under the most favorable conditions, and it certainly will never come to pass until individualism of effort is encouraged and personal energy rewarded.

It is also true that if the Russian people should be converted into an industrial and economic organization it would be necessary to gather them into

towns and cities, to concentrate their labor, and
to educate them. Nor more than three per cent
of the moujiks, it is said — and correctly, I believe
— can now read or write. There are newspapers
printed in Moscow, but I never saw one sold on
the streets, nor did I see anybody reading one, and
the signs on the shops which appeal for the trade
of the masses are largely pictorial. To make such
a people economic and industrial, they must be educated, organized, and quickened. When that is
done, the docile peasant, with his depressed look,
his quiet ways, and his simple faith in God and
the Tsar, will have disappeared. His place will
be taken by the active and energetic workingman,
and the present system of autocracy will come to
a speedy end. Whether this change can be wrought
in the character of the Russian is doubtful, but
if it can be effected it would take a long time, and
no effort is now being made to bring it about.
Perhaps those who control the destinies of Russia
perceive that securing industrial success after the
Western fashion requires a change in the character
and training of the people which would involve
a revolution in the forms of government; but
whether they see it or not, they are making no
effort to advance their people in that way. The
great body of the Russians, consisting of the peasant
and farmer classes, are fettered hand and foot by

the communal land tenure and by the burden of payments, which they are forced to make for the lands which they formerly worked as serfs. This constitutes an absolutely insurmountable barrier at present to their advancement. They have, moreover, no outlet for their products, because there is no system of distribution sufficient to their needs, and there is no encouragement whatever to individual progress and personal effort.

Russian statesmen are not blind to the perils of the existing situation; and if they are not seeking to give opportunity to individualism, they are at least trying to secure, in their own socialistic way, industrial development for Russia. This is the controlling idea of M. Witte, the Minister of Finance, who is to-day the strongest man and the dominating force in the public life of Russia. He sees very plainly the vital necessity of industrial development, and he is trying to secure it through the Government. To Americans the effort, powerful and well directed as it is, seems painfully hopeless. The Government undertakes to run not only the railroads and the telegraphs, but it regulates sugar production and interferes directly with all the industrial activities of the country. The banks are urged to lend money for the assistance of industries. The industries expand beyond their strength and fail. The banks are threatened with disaster, and fall back upon the Government.

The Government sustains the banks and turns to western Europe and to America for loans. If the loans fail — and sooner or later borrowing for enterprises which do not pay must come to an end — the machinery of business will stop. Such a system, no matter how energetically it is pressed, cannot sustain itself or hope to compete in the long run with the highly organized and thoroughly economical systems of other countries like France and Germany, or like England and the United States.

With patience and tenacity of purpose, with courage and much governing capacity, Russia has gone on adding one great region after another to her possessions. She has shown two leading qualities of a ruling race in her ability to expand and govern; but when the territory comes into her possession, no matter how rich it is, she either cannot develop it at all or at best only partially and unprofitably. Her own original territory is still undeveloped and unorganized, and what is true of European Russia is true also of her great Eastern possessions. It is useless, economically speaking, to acquire territory if nothing can be done to improve it; if it cannot be made a benefit either to its own inhabitants or to the country which has taken possession of it. Every acre of land that Russia now adds is a weakness. Her undeveloped territory involves an immense burden of expense, and a great deal of it practically yields nothing. The point has been reached when the more she adds to her domain the essentially weaker she grows. There is but one remedy, and that is to develop the personal energy and industrial force of the people, if they possess these qualities. It will certainly be a slow process, but it is the only one which will succeed. Russia cannot use her vast resources; cannot survive under modern conditions in the long run by any of the devices of a military socialism. While she is as she is, the better organized nations have nothing to fear from her trade competition. She can bar them out from the vast regions under her sway, but she can win no share of the world's trade, and she cannot apparently build up a domestic trade and industry of serious importance. She has an immense domain, she is potentially a great force of the future, but all this force will rust unused unless it can be grasped by the masses of the people, who must then adapt themselves to the modern conditions, under which survival is alone possible.

The work of diplomacy and the ability to govern in which the statesmen of Russia have shown themselves masters, a powerful army, judicious alliances, and a patient, obstinate adhesion to well-matured plans can do much, can make Russia, as they have made her, formidable to all her neighbors and a great power in Europe and Asia. But farther than this she cannot go, no position less precarious than that of to-day can she occupy, until the energies of her people are called out and given full play.   If these energies, once set free to hope and strive, prove to be capable of high economic development, then she can look forward to winning a position as a world-power commensurate with her vast resources and perilous, indeed, to all her rivals.   Unless all the teachings of history and science are vain, there is no other way.

ROCHAMBEAU [1]

Statecraft has a cynical maxim that there is no such thing as gratitude between nations. If we must accept this as true of those practical dealings where sentiment comes into hopeless collision with self-interest, we may at least say that no nation really great will ever hesitate to make public acknowledgment of its obligations to others in the past. The New World of North America has had a long and close connection with the people of France. At the very dawn of the sixteenth century Breton fishermen had followed in the track of the Cabots, and were plying their dangerous trade off the coast of Newfoundland. Thirty years later Cartier was in the St. Lawrence laying the foundation of New France by the mighty river of the North. When the century had just passed its meridian, the Huguenots came to Florida, and the great name of Coligny links itself with our history as the inspirer of distant expeditions to the untrodden shores of America, even when France herself was torn with the wars of religion. It is a dark and

[1] Address delivered at the Unveiling of the Statue of the Comte de Rochambeau, Washington, May 24, 1902.

splendid story, wellnigh forgotten now, which comes
up to us out of that dim past touched with the glory
of the admiral of France.   There in the old books we
can read of Ribault and Laudonnière and their com-
rades, of their daring and intelligence, and of the
settlements they founded.   Then come Menendez and
his Spaniards, the surprise and slaughter of the
French, massacred on account of their religion; and
then, a few years later, De Gourgues swoops down
upon the Spanish forts, and the Spaniards in turn
drench the sands with their blood and swing on gibbets
to remind all men of the passing of the avenger.   Thus
driven from the South, the French still held their grip
on the heritage of Cartier.   Champlain gave his name
to the great lake of New England, where rival nations
were one day to fight for dominion.   French missionaries died for their faith among the red men of
New York.   Père Marquette explored the West, and
the gallant La Salle bore the lilies of France from
the source to the mouth of the Mississippi.   The
French names mark the passing of the French dis-
coverers from Montreal to St. Louis and from St.
Louis to New Orleans.   And while the "Roi Soleil"
was raising his frowning fortress on the banks of the
St. Lawrence, despatching Auvergnats and Normans
and Bretons to settle Canada and urging his explor-
ers across the continent, some others of his best subjects, driven forth into the world by revoked edicts

and certain things called dragonnades, were bringing
their wit and quick intelligence to strengthen and
upbuild the English colonies, which were growing up
not at all in the orderly way dear to the heart of a
grand monarch, but in a rude, vigorous, scrambling,
independent fashion, after the manner of races who
found nations and establish states.

Presently it appeared that there was not room
enough even in the vast wildernesses of North
America for the rival powers of France and England.
A few shots fired by sundry Virginians under the
command of George Washington, whose name, spring-
ing forth suddenly from the backwoods, was then first
heard in two continents, began a stubborn war, which
ended only with the fall of the French power and
the triumph of England and the English colonies.
Thus was a new situation created in North America.
Instead of two rival powers struggling for mastery,
one reigned supreme from the St. Lawrence to Florida.
The danger from the North, dark with Indian warfare, which had so long threatened the Atlantic
colonies, had passed away. The need of the strong
support of the mother country against the power of
France had gone, and the position of the colonies in their
relations with England was enormously strengthened.
A blundering ministry, a few meddlesome and oppres-
sive acts on the part of Parliament, a departure from
Walpole's wise maxim about America, " Quieta non

movere," and mischief would be afoot. It all came
sooner than any one dreamed. The rejoicings at the
close of the victorious war had hardly ended, the
congratulations to the " Great Commoner" had
hardly ceased, the statue of George III. was scarcely
firm on its pedestal, when the Americans rose in
wrath against the Stamp Act. England gave way
sufficiently to make the colonies realize their power,
and yet not so completely as to extinguish suspicion
and hostility. There was a lull, a period of smiling,
deceptive calm, then the storm broke again, and this
time there was not wisdom enough left in London to
allay it. The little minds which Burke thought so
ill suited to a great empire were in full control, and
the empire began in consequence to show an ominous
and ever-widening rent.

Again France appears upon the continent where for
so many years she had played such a great part, and
had fought so bravely and so unavailingly for dominion. The chance had come to wreak an ample ven-
geance upon the power which had driven her from
Canada. France would have been more or less than
human if she had not grasped the opportunity at
once so satisfying to wounded pride and so promising
politically. Covertly at first she aided the English
colonies, and then after the surrender of Burgoyne at
Saratoga, the treaty of alliance was signed, and
France entered into the war with Great Britain.

The French government aided us with money and with men, by land and by sea, but the decisive force was that which landed at Newport in the long July days of 1780.

To that brave, well-officered, highly disciplined army we raise a monument to day, by placing here in the nation's capital the statue of its commander. For their service and for his own we owe him a debt of gratitude, for which we would here make lasting acknowledgment, one which will stand unchanged beneath the sunshine and the rain long after the words we speak shall have been forgotten.

This statue is the counterfeit presentment of the gallant figure of a gallant gentleman. Born in 1725, of noble family, a native of Vendôme, Jean Baptiste Donatien de Vimeur, Comte de Rochambeau, had just passed his fifty-fifth birthday when he landed at Newport. His career had been long and distinguished. His honors and his rank in the army had been won in the field, not in the antechambers of Versailles. In an age when the greatest noblemen of France thought it no shame to seek advancement from royal mistresses by whose whims ministers rose and fell and the policies of state were decided, Rochambeau in time of peace turned from the court to his regiment and his estates. He had shared in all the campaigns of France from the time when his elder brother's death had taken him from the church, in which he was about to become a priest, and placed him in the army. At the siege of Namur he earned the rank of colonel by the surprise of an outpost which led to the surrender of the town. He was twice wounded at the head of his regiment at the battle of Laufeld. He captured the enemy's magazines at the siege of Maestricht, and won the Cross of St. Louis leading the assault upon the forts of Minorca. He fought the Prince Ferdinand of Brunswick, and captured the fortress of Regenstein in 1757. At Crefeld he sustained for a long time the attack of the Prussian army; he took a leading part in the battle of Minden, and was again wounded at Kloster camp. After the peace Rochambeau was often consulted by ministers, but never would take office. At last, in March, 1780, he was made lieutenant-general and sent with the French army to America.

He reached the United States at a dark hour for the American cause. The first fervor of resistance had cooled, the active fighting had subsided in the North, Congress had grown feeble and inert, government and finance both dragged heavily, and it seemed as if the Revolution, so successful in the field, would founder upon the rocks of political and executive incapacity. Washington and the army, in the midst of almost unparalleled difficulties, alone kept the cause alive. The coming of Rochambeau and his men was a great good fortune, and yet its first result was to induce further relaxation of effort on the part of Congress. Washington, realizing all the event meant, opened correspondence at once with Rochambeau, but it was not until September that he was able to seek the French commander in person at Hartford. It was a great relief to the heavily burdened general to meet such a man as Rochambeau, and yet even then, as he turned back with lightened heart and lifted hopes, the news of Arnold's treason smote him on his arrival at West Point.

So the summer had gone and nothing had been done. Then Rochambeau was unwilling to move without further reinforcements, and Washington was struggling desperately to wring from a hesitating Congress and from reluctant States the men, money, and supplies absolutely essential if the great opportunity which had now come was not to pass away unused. So the winter wore on and spring came, and in May Washington and Rochambeau were again in consultation. Washington was determined to strike a fatal blow somewhere. He considered Florida and the scheme of taking the British under Rawdon in the rear; he thought of Virginia, where Cornwallis, forced northward by Green's stratagem, was established with his army; long and earnestly he looked at New York, the chief seat of British power. Rochambeau showed his military intelligence by leaning strongly to Virginia. But the one vital condition was still lacking: Washington knew that he must command the sea, if only for a month, at the point where he was to deliver the decisive blow. So the days slipped by, the summer waned, and then of a sudden the great condition sprang into life. De Grasse, to whom we owe a debt as great as to Rochambeau, appeared in the Chesapeake with his fleet. No longer was there room for doubt. Cornwallis in Virginia was clearly now the quarry for the allied forces.

Time forbids me to tell the brilliant story of that campaign; of the manner in which De Barras was induced to bring his squadron from the north; of the adroitness with which Clinton was deceived in New York; of the skill and rapidity with which the French and American armies were hurried from New York to the Chesapeake, and thence to Yorktown. The great, the golden moment so longed for by Washington, when he could unite both land and sea power, had at last arrived. De Grasse was master of the bay. The English fleet was scattered and divided. Clinton slumbered in New York, and Cornwallis, with some 9,000 men, was in Yorktown, with the united French and American armies drawn close about him. Fast followed the siege, nearer came the enclosing lines; Lauzun dashed back Tarle-

ton's cavalry at the very beginning, and every British
sortie from that moment was repulsed. Day by day
the parallels were pushed forward, and at last Washington declared the advanced British redoubts prac-
ticable for assault. The French, under Vioménil,
the Grenadiers of Gatinois, the regiments of Auvergne and Deux-Ponts stormed one, and here the
most famous of the French regiments recovered from
their king the proud motto of "Auvergne sans
tache." The other redoubt was assigned to the
Americans under Lafayette, led by Alexander Hamilton and John Laurens. Both assaults, brilliantly
delivered, were successful, and the American lines
included the ground which had been so gallantly
won. A desperate sortie under Colonel Graham completely repulsed, a vain attempt to escape by water,
and then all was over. On the 18th of October
Cornwallis surrendered, and on the following day
the British filed out and laid down their arms,
passing between the ordered lines of the French
drawn up under the lilies and the ranks of the
Americans standing beneath the thirteen stars fixed
on that day in the firmanent of nations. The
American Revolution had been fought out and the
new people had won.

Through all these events, through all the months
of weary waiting, through the weeks of rapid march
and the hurrying days of siege and battle, there shine

out very brightly the fine qualities of the French general. Nothing is more difficult than the management in war of allied forces. Here there was never a jar. Rochambeau was large-minded enough to understand the greatness of Washington, to realize the height of mind and the power of character which invested the American leader with a dignity beyond aught that royal birth or kingly title could confer. No small jealousies marred their intercourse. They wrought together for a common cause; and the long experience, the thorough training, the keen military intelligence, the wisdom and honest purpose of Rochambeau were all freely given to the Americans and their commander. Honor and gratitude, then, to Rochambeau for what he did for us, and gratitude and honor likewise to De Grasse and De Barras for the sea power with which they upheld and sustained both Washington and Rochambeau.

But there is something more in the story than this; something of deeper meaning than the plans of statesmen to humble a successful foe and take a tardy revenge for past defeats; something more profound than the grasping of a young people at a friendly hand to draw them forth from the stormy waters of a desperate war for liberty. Look again on those men gathered under the white flag in the mellow October sunlight. The pride of victory is in their hearts, for they have done well for France; they have cruelly

avenged the loss of Canada. The world smiles upon
them as the British pass by and pile their arms.
Happily for them they cannot read the future. They
do not even grasp the meaning of the war they have
helped to bring to an end. They cannot interpret

" Time's dark events
Charging like ceaseless clouds across the sky."

But their future is our past, and we know their
destinies. There is Rochambeau himself, chief figure
among the French. He will go home to added honors;
he will take part presently in the movement for reform, and will receive from a new government a
marshal's baton. Then a torrent of blood flows.
Others of his rank will fly across the frontier, but he
is made of sterner stuff. He will retire to his estates,
be dragged to prison, will be barely saved from the
guillotine by the Ninth Thermidor, and will live on
to receive the compliments of the greatest soldier of
modern times, and will die full of years and honors.
There is Lafayette. For him an Austrian prison is
waiting. There is Vioménil, who commanded the
force which took the redoubt. He will die in hiding,
wounded in defence of his king's palace against the
onset of a maddened people on the 10th of August.
There is Damas, wounded at the Yorktown redoubt.
In a few years he will be a fugitive and an exile
fighting against France. There is Lameth, wounded

also at the redoubt. For him, too, the future holds a prison and a long exile. There is Lauzun, type of the *ancien régime*, the victor over Tarleton's horse, the bearer of the brave news to Versailles; he, too, will stay by France, and his end will be the guillotine. The prophet who should have foretold such fates as these for that gallant company would have been laughed to scorn. From no men did disaster seem more distant than from those brave gentlemen of France on that October morning, and yet the future held for them exile, prison, and the guillotine. And it was all inevitable, for the American Revolution not only made a new nation, but it was the beginning of a world-wide movement, at once mighty and relentless. There was something stronger than government or ministers, than kings or politics, which brought the French to America.

Across the square stands the statue of Lafayette. He brought to America no army like Rochambeau, no fleet like De Grasse. He came by no command of his king. Yet has he always been nearer to the hearts of the Americans than any man not of their own people. The reason is not far to seek. He came of his own accord, and brought with him the sympathy of France. He represented the new spirit of a new time, the aspirations, the hopes, the visions which had come out of the intellectual revolution wrought by Voltaire, Rousseau, and the Encyclopédistes. Purposes of state, calculations of chances, selfish desires might guide the French Government, but Lafayette was the living embodiment of the sympathy of the French people for the cause of the United States. He came because he loved that cause and had faith in it, and so the American people gave faith and love to him. And this impalpable spirit of the time, stirring strongly but blindly in France, was even then more powerful than monarchs or cabinets or coalitions. In America it passed for the first time from the world of speculation to the world of action. There in the new country, on the edge of the yet unconquered continent, theory became practice and doctrines lived as facts. There a people had risen up declaring that they were weary of kings, had fought their own battle for their own hand, and won. The democratic movement had begun.

From America it passed across the sea, saying to all men that what had been done in the new land could be done likewise in the old. The army of Rochambeau, flushed with victory, bore back the message with them, and it fell upon listening ears. France had helped us to liberty and independence, and we had shown her how both were won. The force which we had summoned they, too, evoked, and banded Europe, blind to the deeper meanings of the American war, went to pieces in dull surprise before the onset of a people armed, the makers of a revolution in which thrones tottered, privilege and feudalism went down to ruin, and the ancient boundaries of kings faded from the map. The lilies which had floated so triumphantly in the Virginian air gave way to the American colors, which French armies carried in triumph from Paris to Moscow, and from the Baltic to the Nile, wiping out forever the petty tyrannies which sold men to fight in quarrels not their own, and clearing the ground for the larger liberty and the united nations of to-day. The United States, with independence achieved, passed out of the network of European politics, in which for a century and a half the American colonies had been entangled, but the influence and example of the American revolution were felt throughout the civilization of the West.

We unveil this statue in honor of a brave soldier who fought by the side of Washington. We place it here to keep his memory fresh in remembrance and as a monument of our gratitude to France. But let us not forget that we also commemorate here the men who first led in arms the democratic movement which during a century of conflict has advanced the cause of freedom and popular government throughout the world of Western civilization.

APPENDIX

LETTER FROM HON. GEORGE F. HOAR

In regard to Mr. Sherman and Mr. Ellsworth and the share of each in securing the " Connecticut Compromise "

ISLES OF SHOALS, July 28, 1902.

MY DEAR COLLEAGUE, — I suppose as a writer and student of American History, dwelling in Boston, you have often been bothered by the claims of your contemporaries in behalf of their grandfathers. On the other hand, as a Bostonian with an illustrious great-grandfather of your own, you must have learned to sympathize with the feeling.

So I make no apology for calling your attention to the question whether Mr. Ellsworth can be justly credited with having designed the existing distribution of political power between the States and the Nation in National Legislation, or of having caused the adoption of the same by his efforts in the Convention that framed the Constitution, or whether, on the other hand, Mr. Sherman is not justly entitled to that credit.

The question is not of very great importance to the fame of either. Each of them rendered enough distinguished public service to bear the subtraction of that from his credit without any serious impairment of his fame. That is especially true of Oliver Ellsworth, who gained so great a distinction in diplomacy, in jurisprudence, in legislation, and as a builder of the Constitution.

I heard your address at New Haven. The subject was very dear to me indeed. I have always felt toward Oliver Ellsworth as you might feel toward a very dear uncle, or, except for the difference in time, as toward an elder brother. He was my grandfather's dearest and closest friend. My mother was constantly in his household, and his daughter was my mother's dearest friend in her youth, and his children were her playmates. So I heard stories about the Ellsworths, or to use my mother's phrase, what " Judge Ellsworth used to say," as you heard stories doubtless from your parents of your grandparents. Ellsworth's great service has been too much neglected by historians. Save the excellent, but of course brief, tribute to him by Mr. Bancroft, there has been no adequate tribute to him until yours.

But I think you will agree that the chief credit of the Connecticut Compromise, as it has been called, does not belong to him.

I have drawn off from the Madison papers everything which was said or done by either of them in regard to the subject. Of all this I send you a copy. The dates are given. The pages referred to are those of the edition just published by Congress, in what is called the " Documentary History of the Constitution of the United States," which I have no doubt you have at hand.

What Mr. Ellsworth said and did in the matter is this. June 11th, he seconded Roger Sherman's motion. This motion was that the proportion of suffrage in the first branch should be according to numbers, and that in the second branch each State should have one vote and no more. That motion was, after debate, lost. June 29th, Mr. Ellsworth moved that the rule of suffrage in the second branch be the same with that established by the Articles of Confederation. He made an able speech, briefly reported, in which he said that he hoped that this would become a ground of compromise in regard to the second branch, and that Massachusetts was the only State to the eastward that would agree to a plan which did not contain this provision. That motion also was lost. June 30th, he made another able speech in favor of that proposition. June 25th, he made another able speech on the same subject.

July 2nd, he was elected to the Committee on Representation in the Senate. He did not serve on the Committee, but was replaced by Mr. Sherman. July 5th, he said he was ready to accede to the compromise they had reported. July 14th, he asked two very searching and pregnant questions of Mr. Wilson and Mr. Madison, the answers to which tended to destroy the force of Mr. Wilson's argument against the compromise. August 8th, Mr. Ellsworth did not think the clause as to originating money bills of any consequence, but as it was thought of consequence by some of the members from the larger States, he was willing that it should stand.

So, to sum up Mr. Ellsworth's work in the matter, he made a motion, which was lost, covering a part of the plan. He seconded Mr. Sherman's original motion, which was lost. He made another motion substantially to the same effect, which was lost, and made three strong speeches and put two pertinent questions on the side of the measure. He was put on the Grand Committee, but did not serve, but afterwards expressed his acquiescence in the report, and was obliged to leave the Convention before it adjourned without signing the Constitution.

Now, on the other hand, see what Mr. Sherman had to do with it, both as to conceiving the plan, and as to promoting its adoption by the Convention after it had been twice rejected. First, you find in John Adams' diary that this same question occasioned a very earnest struggle in the Continental Congress. I have not the references at hand, but you will easily find them by looking at the index of John Adams' works.[1] John Adams says that in 1776, Mr. Sherman being on the Committee to frame the Articles of Confederation, Mr. Sherman wanted to have the question taken both ways, the States first to vote according to numbers and again on the principle of equality, and that no vote should be deemed to be carried unless it had a majority vote both ways.

This is in substance what Mr. Sherman moved first in the Constitutional Convention.

That this was a subject of great discussion and controversy in the Congress, and considered of the most vital importance, is clear, not only from the character of the question, but from Dr. Franklin's statement made in the Constitutional Convention as to what happened in the Continental Congress in 1774. Mr. Sherman was a member of that Congress, as he was of the Congress in 1776. Mr. Ellsworth was not a member of the Continental Congress in either of those years.

So Mr. Sherman had been through one great contest on this same question, and had himself devised the solution which was finally in substance adopted in the Constitution.

Next, Mr. Sherman made the first motion for the adoption of this principle in the Convention, June 11th. The relation of that motion to the old controversy in the Continental Congress appears clearly from the fact that Dr. Franklin's statement on that subject was made to the Convention the same day.

Also on the same day, Mr. Sherman, having made his original proposition, moved that the question be taken upon it and declared that everything depended upon that. He

[1] Works of John Adams, vol. ii. pp. 365 ff., 496–501.

declared that the smaller States would never agree to the plan on any other principle than an equality of suffrage in this branch.

This, as appears above, was June 11th. Mr. Ellsworth took no part in the matter, except seconding Mr. Sherman's motion, until June 29th. June 20th, Mr. Sherman made a long and strong speech in favor of the plan. June 28th also, Mr. Sherman made another earnest speech in favor of the plan. So he had not only devised the scheme, but moved it in the Convention, and made three speeches in its favor before Mr. Ellsworth was heard from. Next, when on July 2nd General Pinckney moved the Grand Committee to devise and report a compromise, Mr. Sherman spoke in favor of the motion. He said, " We are now at a full stop, and nobody he supposed meant that we should break up without doing something." Mr. Ellsworth took no part in that.

July 2nd, Mr. Ellsworth was elected on the Committee. But he went off the Committee alleging indisposition, and Mr. Sherman went on. The indisposition could not have been very serious because Mr. Ellsworth is found taking part in the proceedings of the Convention, I think, without intermission. He was present in the Convention, and spoke July 5th, the first day of their meeting after the Committee was appointed. So it seems not unlikely that his indisposition was not only not very serious, but that he went off the Committee in order that Mr. Sherman, who had shown such great interest in the matter, should take his place. But this of course is mere conjecture and is not entitled to much weight.

Mr. Sherman then appears as moving in the Committee a further limitation on the power of the Senate, namely, that while the House was to vote according to numbers, no measure should pass the Senate unless there was a majority

in the Senate as representing population, and also a majority
as representing the States in its favor. Mr. Madison says
that that was not much deliberated upon or approved. It
does not affect the point we are dealing with one way or the
other. But it seems to me likely that Mr. Madison, who did
not himself attend the meeting of the Committee, probably
got his information from somebody who misapprehended the
point, because it does not seem likely that that proposition
would have been made. If Mr. Sherman made any motion
at all of the sort, I should conjecture that it was one which was
expected to take effect only in case the old plan of a single
branch, or of amending the Articles of Confederation, which
both he and Ellsworth as well as Patterson and some others
had favored, were adopted. But this is all idle conjecture.

After the Committee had been appointed Mr. Sherman, on
the 7th of July, makes a speech at some length in favor of the
plan. Mr. Ellsworth did nothing further, except his speech
and questions on July 14th. On July 14th, Mr. Rutledge
moved to reconsider the two propositions touching the originating of money bills in the first and equality of votes in the
second branch. Mr. Sherman replied to him and objected,
but the objections seemed to have been waived, and Mr.
Sherman made another speech, so that he spoke twice on
that day. September 5th, Gouverneur Morris moved to post-
pone the clause concerning money bills which formed part of
the Compromise. Mr. Sherman replied to him that he was
for giving immediate ease to those who look on this clause as
of great moment, and for trusting to their concurrence in
other proper measures.

Now it seems to me, from the foregoing summary, that Mr.
Sherman, besides having devised and proposed the measure,
and having made more speeches than any other person in its
favor, may be fairly considered to have been the member who

had the measure in charge. He undertakes to speak for the smaller States, and whenever any question of postponing or proceeding to consider or reconsider is made he arises to represent his side. Not only that, but when Mr. Morris tries to get rid of the clause about Money Bills which had been desired by the larger States, and also was advocated later by General Washington in the only speech he made as to any provision of the Constitution as being of great importance, Mr. Sherman insisted that that should be disposed of, and that those who favored it should be trusted to concur in other proper measures; but finally, and what seems to me a clincher, on the 15th of September, when the provision as to amending the Constitution was up, Mr. Sherman moved what nobody of the small States seems to have thought of before, to annex to the end of the articles a further proviso, that no State shall, without its consent, be affected in its internal police, or be deprived of its equal suffrage in the Senate. That was lost. Mr. Sherman then instantly moved to strike out the provision authorizing amendments to the Constitution altogether. That was lost. But there were such murmurs of discontent among the representatives of the small States that the majority yielded, and Morris, who had himself strenuously resisted the whole arrangement, moved to annex the further proviso that no state, without its consent, shall be deprived of its equal suffrage in the Senate. This was unanimously agreed to. This motion of Gouverneur Morris was only a repetition of Mr. Sherman's motion without the provision as to internal police. This was the last day of the Convention, and no further action was taken except the signature of the members.

So it seems to me clear that the plan was Mr. Sherman's, that the proposal of it in the Convention was Mr. Sherman's, that the first motion in its favor was Mr. Sherman's, and that the final proposition which made it safe in the clause about amending the Constitution was Mr. Sherman's; and that he was on the Committee that reported it, and that he made more speeches in its favor than anybody else, and seems to have had the entire management or conduct of the measure.

On the other hand, Mr. Ellsworth's contribution was seconding Mr. Sherman's first motion, making a similar motion himself, which was lost, and three or four powerful speeches in its favor.

Now I know very well that there are many cases where one man will move a measure, will propose and devise a measure, and will even have charge of a measure in a legislative body when the success of the measure is due to the powerful influence of another. I suppose if some resolution declaring the doctrine of Webster's reply to Hayne had been moved by Mr. Foote or somebody else, and had been adopted by the Senate, that Webster would have been the man to whom the securing of the adoption would be due. I suppose that the success of Hamilton's financial policy is due to him, and not to the men who introduced or supported it, in either House of Congress.

You and I have seen many examples like the first in our own experience. I have prided myself a good deal on the provision for succession to the Executive power which was substituted for the old, clumsy arrangement, but I should have been in very great danger of losing it by the adoption of an amendment which would have spoiled it, by requiring a Presidential election to be had at once in the case that the bill provided for, but for Mr. Evarts coming to my help in a powerful speech which convinced and carried the Senate.

But I do not think that can be said as to the comparative influence of Mr. Sherman and Mr. Ellsworth, great as was the power of the latter.

Mr. Sherman, if he were remarkable for anything, was remarkable for his great tenacity in insisting on plans he had once devised, his great success in attaining his objects, and his great influence over the bodies to which he belonged, especially his great influence over the minds of the ablest men. I think he may be fairly compared to Alexander Hamilton in that particular. That this is true is proved by abundant testimonials from his great contemporaries. I do not think such testimonials are in existence in regard to another of them save Washington alone, with a possible exception of Dr. Franklin. I cite a few of them from memory. Theodore Sedgwick, who served with Mr. Sherman in Washington's first administration, said: "He was the man of the selectest wisdom he ever knew. His influence was such, in the bodies to which he belonged, that he never failed to carry every measure and every part of a measure which he advocated." I do not think the record will support this statement of Theodore Sedgwick's to its full extent, but it will support it almost to its full extent.

Fisher Ames said "that if he happened to be out of his seat when a subject was discussed, and came in when the question was about to be taken, he always felt safe in voting as Mr. Sherman did, for he always voted right." Patrick Henry said that the first men in the Continental Congress were Washington, Richard Henry Lee, and Roger Sherman. He said at another time that Roger Sherman and George Mason were the greatest statesmen he ever knew. This statement appears in Howe's "Historical Collections of Virginia," in the Life of George Mason, and in the Life of Patrick Henry. I took pains to verify it by writing to William Wirt Henry, Patrick Henry's grandson. I have his letter in my possession in which he declares that there is no doubt about it. He has frequently heard his mother, who was Patrick Henry's daughter-in-law, and in whose household Patrick Henry lived in his old age, state the fact, and especially he got from his mother an account of Howe's visit to his father and mother, not long after Patrick Henry's death, when Mr. Howe received the statement from Patrick Henry's son and his wife, William Wirt Henry's parents.

John Adams said of him that " he was one of the soundest and strongest pillars of the Revolution," and that he never knew two men more alike than Sherman and Ellsworth, except that the Chief Justice had the advantage of a liberal education. General Scott, who, with all his foibles, was a very great master of constitutional principles, said that he thought Roger Sherman was entitled to be considered as the fourth man in the transactions embracing the whole Revolutionary period and the formation of the new government. John Adams spoke of him on another occasion, in a letter to his wife, " as firm in the cause of American Independence as Mt. Atlas." Mr. Jefferson pointed him out to Dr. Spring, and said, " That is Mr. Sherman of Connecticut, a man who never said a foolish thing in his life."

I hope you will not think that I quote these things from the vanity of a near relative, but it seems important to this particular question to see whether, after all, whatever might have been Mr. Sherman's original relation to the matter, Mr. Ellsworth's superior strength and influence may not entitle him to the credit of its accomplishment. However, I do not think I need to cite much stronger evidence on this point than that of Judge Ellsworth himself, who paid to Mr. Sherman the high tribute you cite in your address, — a tribute which was never paid by any public man to another on any other occasion that I know, — that he had formed his own character on Mr. Sherman's model. It may possibly be worth while to add to what I have said, that Mr. Sherman

never during his long life failed of re-election to any public office that he held, except in the case of the Connecticut
legislature in the early days, where the principle of rotation
in office was firmly established. When after the Revolutionary War there was danger that a Tory would be elected
the first Mayor of New Haven, Mr. Sherman, though then
absent, I think, at the Constitutional Convention, was chosen
Mayor. Thereupon the legislature passed a law that the
office of Mayor should be held at the pleasure of the legislature. That resulted, as it was intended, in a life tenure of
office for Mr. Sherman. He held the office of Mayor until
he died, although during the same period he served as Representative in Congress and as Senator.

So, while Mr. Ellsworth's great character and ability as
shown by his other public employments is unquestioned, it
can hardly be claimed that he should have the credit of a
measure, otherwise apparently due to Mr. Sherman, by reason
that his strength was needed to its success.

I hope that I have not wearied you by this discussion, or
trespassed too much on your good nature. But I think you
will like to be sure, in publishing what I am confident is to
be a historical paper of very great and permanent value, to
get right in every detail. I am, with highest regard,

Faithfully yours,

GEORGE F. HOAR.

N.B. In summing up Ellsworth's and Sherman's contributions to this debate in this letter, I only included
speeches that bear on the point of the Compromise, namely,
the voting according to the principle of equality in one
branch and according to numbers in the other, and giving to
the House the exclusive power to originate money bills.
There are several speeches by Ellsworth, as there are by

Patterson of New Jersey, in favor of the equality of the States, and in favor of engrafting the new provision and the old confederation. That also was the idea of Mr. Sherman before the Convention met. There is now in existence in his handwriting, in the possession of my cousin at New Haven, the papers which he took with him to the Convention, proposing his scheme of a Constitution. That is copied in Boutell's Life of Roger Sherman. I have in my possession a copy of the Constitution wholly in his handwriting, as it appeared shortly after the report of the Grand Committee. It was altered considerably after that time.